SKIPPING AUGUST

RICHA FRESHLEY

Copyright © 2018 Richa Freshley

All rights reserved. No part of this publication may be reproduced, distributed, or transmitted in any form or by any means, including photocopying, recording, or other electronic or mechanical methods, without the prior written permission of the publisher, except in the case of brief quotations embodied in critical reviews and certain other noncommercial uses permitted by copyright law. For permission requests, please write to the author, addressed "Attention: Permissions," at the address below.

Contents

PREFACE 1
CHAPTER 1 - HEADING BACK TO CALI 2
CHAPTER 2 - CODE BLUE 27
CHAPTER 3 – TICK TOCK, TICK TOCK 40
CHAPTER 4 – ROAD TO RECOVERY 61
CHAPTER 5 – NOW I LAY YOU DOWN TO SLEEP 68
CHAPTER 6 – BACK TO REALITY 77
CHAPTER 7 – THE CARRIER 87
CHAPTER 8 – INVISIBLE WINGS 91
CHAPTER 9 – THE TRUTH 104
CHAPTER 10 – CHAOS 112
CHAPTER 11 – GOD's WHISPER 126
CHAPTER 12 - THE GIFT 131
CHAPTER 13 - SOUL SEARCHING 135
CHAPTER 14 - HAPPILY EVER AFTER 152
REFERENCES 161

PREFACE

Ten years ago, my journey began when I delivered a stillborn baby girl. This spiraled me into coding on the table for 90 minutes from an amniotic fluid embolism which put me into full cardiac arrest because of a side effect from an off-label drug. It is a journey that has taken me ten years to write. I was angry, depressed, couldn't trust, lost part of my memory, cheated death only to ask, "Why me?" But through this journey, I found true love. I began to heal, I forgave, I got stronger and now my story has changed from "Why me" to a loving and compassionate "Why *not* me?" I'm a small-town girl whose dream was to be a mother and to know love. Today, I'm a successful business owner, a mother and a wife. My life feels complete except for telling this story. I hope it inspires, teaches and helps you through the challenging times that life can throw at you—with the promise to live *your* life because tomorrow, unlike yesterday, is never guaranteed.

CHAPTER 1 - HEADING BACK TO CALI

It's Thursday August 21st, 2008 and we're heading back to Cali. My husband, my son Nixon who is two-years-old and me—we're on our way to beautiful Laguna Beach to attend my best friend Stacy's wedding. My husband and I are both from Southern California. He is from San Diego and I am from Costa Mesa, but we are now living in Oklahoma. I was 28 weeks pregnant with a healthy baby girl. I looked like I was having twins, which also happened with my first pregnancy with Nixon. Before leaving, I checked with my doctor to make sure that it was safe for me to fly, as I had been told about some airline restrictions for pregnant women flying. I weighed 200lbs the day I gave birth to Nixon and I was already gaining weight rapidly with this pregnancy—I was

18 7lbs at only 28 weeks! Since my husband and I were from California, we flew into San Diego Airport where his parents, live and they picked us up.

Nixon was such a great traveler, he loved to look out the window at the clouds and was fascinated with everything to do with flying. This was a short trip away from home due to my husband and I not being able to take much time off work. Friday August 22nd was the rehearsal dinner, held in Newport Beach, the city neighboring my home town. We spent Thursday night in San Diego, then Friday morning we had to be in Orange County, so we went to my husband's aunt's house to pick up her BMW convertible that we were borrowing to start the wedding festivities. It was awesome driving from San Diego to Newport Beach in a convertible on the Pacific Coast Highway, just like old times.

Stacy and I have been friends for over 35 years and she chose me to be her maid of honor. I hated leaving Nixon overnight and very rarely did, unless it was with his grandparents, so Nixon went with his grandparents. Since they live out of state and see him only twice a year, this was a good opportunity for them to spend some quality time together.

The rehearsal dinner was held at a restaurant called The Chicken Coop. On our way there my husband and I stopped for gas. I can't recall what started the argument, but my husband and I ended up in a colossal fight. This was a very common occurrence in our marriage, especially lately. I am known to be quite the actress in hiding my feelings, and I did not want anyone to know that my husband and I were not getting along when we arrived, so I covered up with a pleasant smile. I especially didn't want to spoil Stacy's weekend.

Apart from my large belly, you wouldn't know I was 28 weeks pregnant. I loved every minute of being pregnant. I was never sick and always had extra energy. At the rehearsal dinner I did get emotional during my speech but that's normal in a situation like that, pregnant or not. I was a hair stylist, so Stacy asked me to help with the hair and makeup for the wedding party. Knowing how early I had to get started, we went to bed early once the rehearsal dinner was over.

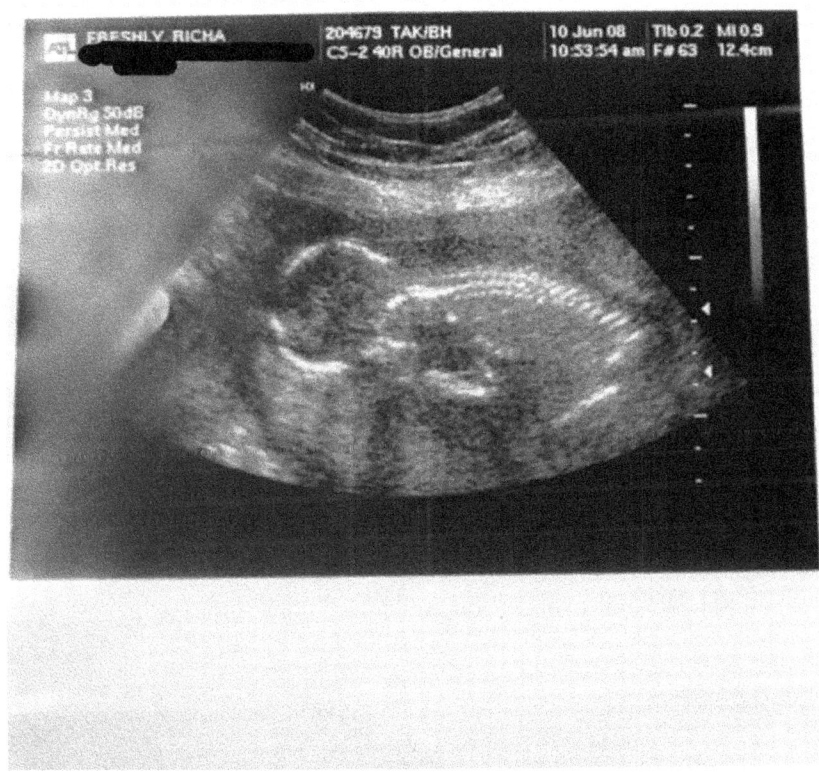

Saturday, August 23rd was the wedding day. The wedding was held in Laguna Beach, a short distance from Newport Beach—although in California driving five miles can take 30 minutes because of the traffic. The ceremony was held at Pacific Edge Beach House in the heart of Laguna.

Pacific Edge Beach House is beautiful. Stacy and Rich were lucky to have their wedding and reception there—it is booked years in advance—and we were lucky to spend the night at the same place the wedding and reception was held. The bridal party wore the same style chocolate brown dresses with a white flower in their hair. I, of course, was the only one pregnant but I still felt beautiful. Stacy was a gorgeous bride, she looked the prettiest I had seen her. After a long busy day of primping and rehearsing, it was time for Stacy and Rich to get married.

The bridesmaids for Stacy's wedding

Stacy and Rich

It was an evening wedding with a sit down formal dinner and a fun reception with lots of alcohol. The one part of being pregnant I disliked was not be able to take part in the fun, such as the champagne toast after the speeches. As everyone hit the dance floor, I was awaiting the father daughter dance of Stacy and her dad. Once announced by the DJ, everyone gathered around the dance floor to watch. As I was brought to tears from happiness, I began to start having a very familiar back pain. The pain suddenly got worse. It was the same pain that I had when I went into pre-labor with my first pregnancy. When that happened, I ended up going to the hospital, where I was given Brethine shots to stop my contractions, because it was too soon for Nixon to be delivered. The shots worked; he stayed where he was, until I was induced a week earlier than his due date. I have a very high tolerance to pain, but now I started to wonder. I thought it was because I had been on my feet since early morning and I was overly tired. I did not want to tell anybody; I just wanted to go up to my room and lie down. The last thing I wanted was to ruin my best friend's wedding by going to the hospital and being told nothing was wrong.

I suffered through the back pain and watched Stacy and her dad's father-daughter dance. Because he was quite a bit older than our friends' dads, it made it even more special that he was still able to dance with her. I am known to leave parties without saying goodbye—I don't want to make a scene—but I remember kissing Stacy on the cheek and telling her I was going to bed. Stacy understood, and I wished her a wonderful wedding night. I told her I would see her in the morning.

Stacy and her Dad

I tried to get comfortable in bed, but it was impossible. The pain was so intense that I needed at least one Tylenol, hoping it would relieve some of the pain. I never took any kind of medication with my first pregnancy or with this one, so I was reluctant to take even one Tylenol, though it is safe.

I woke up in the middle of the night needing to use the restroom, but there was a problem. On our floor there was only one bathroom, and it was in the bridal suite. I prayed to God that I was not about to walk in on Stacy and Rich's wedding night. I tiptoed the best I could on the tile floors, but when I opened the door I heard Stacy yell, "Is that you Richa?" I said "Yes! I have to pee really bad, I'm so sorry I'll be really quick." She asked how I was feeling and I told her much better, which was not a lie. The Tylenol must have kicked in and I was able to go back to bed and get some rest.

The next morning, I was not awakened, as usual, by my daughter's kicks and punches inside my belly. That had become a regular routine about 20 weeks into my pregnancy. My daughter was a constant mover, especially in the mornings when she was most active. Since it had been 48 hours since I had seen Nixon, I missed him terribly and just wanted to get back to San Diego as soon as possible to pick him up and catch our flight home. My husband and I had to be back at work first thing on Monday, so we were going to catch the last flight out of San Diego on Sunday evening.

As the afternoon came and went with no movement from Ellison, I was beginning to feel a little concerned, but I didn't let the concern linger. We made our flight and arrived back at my home town. Monday morning came, and again there had been no movement from my daughter. A growing panic gripped me. To be honest I had shared my concern about Ellison with no one, not even my husband. This shows how disconnected our marriage was at that time.

I ended up at work on Monday and had a full day of clients scheduled. Another hairstylist at the salon I worked at named Carly, a friend of mine, was on a break; we were both waiting for our next clients. I decided to share my concern with her. I had to tell someone, I was freaking out and since she is a mom of two daughters I felt comfortable telling her. She asked me when my next doctor's appointment was, and I told her it was tomorrow. She said in her opinion Ellison was probably running out of room since I was in my last trimester. Because I had a doctor's appointment the next day she told me to wait it out until then. She was there at the perfect time, to tell my worries to and help calm my nerves.

My husband was a better father than husband for me. He was very connected when I was pregnant and wanted to come to every doctor's appointment with both pregnancies. But since we had just got back from vacation, I told him there was no need to come to my Tuesday afternoon doctor's appointment, it was just supposed to be a normal routine 28-week check-up. Maybe the real reason I did not want him there was just in case my worries were confirmed.

He dropped me off for the appointment and I walked into the doctor's office. I knew the receptionist and most of the staff very well because my OBGYN had been a friend since I moved to Oklahoma in 1996. I told my husband I would text him when I was done and that it shouldn't be long.

The waiting room was crowded, but I sighed with relief when I looked around and didn't recognize anyone. I did not know what anxiety felt like, but I felt like I was starting to feel it as I sat down and waited for my turn. I flipped through ten magazines, skimming articles to keep me busy and my mind in control. Anita, my doctor's nurse, called my name; she knows me very well, our husbands worked together. Again, I had that same "smile" on my face and my actress attitude on until we entered the exam room. Alone in the room with Anita, I shared my concern of no movement now for over 72 hours. All the other questions she asked, I answered normally. She told me that the doctor would be in in a minute and that she was sure everything would be just fine.

My doctor knocked on the door and came in. We started our normal chat about life, I do his wife's hair every six weeks and his daughter is a friend of mine. His wife has been a client of mine since beauty school, my longest standing client ever. She is one of the kindest and most generous people I know. I then shared my fears with him and he said, "Well, let's check everything out." If you have never been pregnant before—I'm not sure at what gestation it changes—but at the beginning of your pregnancy you get a vaginal ultrasound, since the baby is so small that is the only way to see your precious baby. Once the baby is bigger, you have a normal ultrasound with the jelly and paddles.

At my last few appointments I was far enough along that all he had to use was a battery-operated heartbeat checker on my outer belly. He would put it on my belly and he would always hear a strong heartbeat right away. He took the heartbeat checker from his coat pocket and put it on the left side of my belly like normal. I watched his face to see his reaction or any indication that there may be a problem. He swiped the heartbeat finder to the right and over to the other side. There was a long pause, then he removed it. He shook it and looked at me. He said he thought the batteries had died and he would be back in a moment.

He might have been gone for only a few minutes, but it seemed like forever. I did not know how to feel at that time, except very alone. I was alone in that room, with awful thoughts going through my head. The doctor walked back into the room and said he could not find any batteries, but he wanted to send me down the hall to have an ultrasound. Blaire was the ultrasound tech, she was also a friend of mine as she was my mom's best friend's sister. The benefits about having a friend that's an ultra sound tech is that I got as many ultrasounds as I wanted throughout my pregnancies, and I could find out the sex as early as possible, and she was always right.

The hallway to the ultrasound room was not long, but as I looked down it, the door to her room seemed miles away. This time I did not want an ultrasound. I knew something was terribly wrong. I stepped into the room with Blaire. My doctor had walked me down the hallway. I looked over to my right and my husband was in the room. I thought to myself

"Why are you here?" and

"How did you get here so fast?"

Blaire asked me to lay on the exam table, so we could look at Ellison. She put the paddle on my stomach, moving it around while staring intensely at the sonogram screen. Just as I had done with my doctor I was watching her face for any signs of a reaction. After a few minutes we made eye contact, she put her head down on my belly and started to cry. My husband was right next to me, holding my hand, and as Blaire laid her head on my stomach, I belted out the loudest scream and cry anyone has ever heard. I know every woman in the waiting room heard it.

My doctor's batteries were not dead. He knew that Ellison's heart had stopped but wanted time to call my husband so he could be there with me when he told us Ellison had passed. As I lay there on the table, I felt numb and still felt alone. I was so confused. I felt that I was a model pregnant mother and I did everything I was told to, nutritionally and safety-wise.

Everything started running through my head. What could I have done to cause this? I did some things during this pregnancy that I didn't do in my first. I took two Tylenol at Stacy's wedding, I had one Coca-Cola, colored my hair, jumped off a diving board, went on a water slide and I rode a go-kart with Nixon. I had also gotten in a car accident. It was just a fender bender and I was fine. I'll never forget as I got out of my car after I was hit by a young college student—he fell to his knees when he realized he had rear-ended a pregnant woman. I helped him up from the ground and told him I was okay, and it was going to be fine. I told him how protected babies are in our bodies and not to worry. What did I do wrong? What did I do to cause Ellison to die?

My doctor tried to reassure me that it was nothing I had done. None of the things I listed could have caused her death and that we wouldn't have any answers until she was delivered. My doctor told us to take a few days to tell our family and friends our situation and we will then decide the method for Ellison's delivery. We left the doctor's office. As Nixon was still at daycare we thought now was the best time to tell my parents. I knew that they were the first people that I wanted to share the sad news with. As we drove up their gravel driveway it seemed like miles. We were both numb, in shock and heartbroken. I felt so bad about the news I was going to share with them. I knew that this was going to break their hearts too.

When we got to the house, I asked them to sit down as we had something important to tell them. We told them where we had just come from and what we were told and that we still had no answers. My mom and dad both cried and hugged us and shared our pain.

The next people we wanted to tell were my husband's parents and his sister who was also five months pregnant. After we told them via phone they too were heartbroken.

They told us they would be on the next flight from California to be with us.

I needed to call my best friend Stacy too. After I did, she told her mom and dad. Bless her mom's soul! She told Stacy that she thought it was because I worked so hard at the wedding and that was why Ellison died. I had to tell her that was not the case and that I am used to working hard.

That night my husband and I didn't sleep a minute. As we lay in bed he asked how long it had been since I felt Ellison move and I told him the truth, about 72 hours. My husband was feeling quite guilty because when we found out our baby was a girl he was slightly disappointed because he wanted another boy because he knew how hard girls were to raise. Before Stacy's wedding, at home in Oklahoma, I remembered the fight we got into, our biggest fight yet. I told him when Ellison was born I was going to divorce him, because of the way I felt I had been treated. We were constantly fighting.

The next morning, I called the owner of the salon where I worked. I told her the news and asked her to pass it on to the rest of the hair stylists. I didn't know when I would be back, but I left them my client book and I knew they would take care of all my clients for me, and they did. It was comforting to know they wanted to support me in any way they could. My home town is a small town and the news spread quickly about my baby.

It is now Thursday, and my doctor called us in to discuss how we would get Ellison out. I hadn't slept at all for days now, I felt very weak and I shared that with him. He gave us three options to deliver Ellison. The first was a C-section. I quickly declined, not wanting to do that method because Nixon was a vaginal birth with no complications and I didn't want a scar to look back on every day to remember it by.

Option two was the drug Pitocin, which is what most women are given to induce labor. With a 28-week fetus, doctors guess how long Pitocin will take to work. It could be a few days or a few weeks. The third option was a drug that my doctor was not familiar with. He admitted that I was the furthest along of a fetal demise that he had dealt with, so he got a second opinion from a specialist in Oklahoma City. He consulted with the high-risk doctor on the best way to get Ellison out and he recommended a different drug that was supposed to be the best option for me in my situation. I trusted my doctor and said that whatever he would recommend if his own daughter was going through this is how I wanted him to get Ellison out.

He told me there were some side effects to this drug. He said severe cramping during the administration of it would occur. The worst-case scenario would be uterine rupture. If that happened I would not be able to have any more children. That side effect was okay with me because if that were to happen and when we would be ready to have another child I would have been fine with adoption. I remember asking him if I was going to die. He assured me I was going to be just fine, but I needed to rest before the delivery.

He told me he would prescribe Ambien, one for that night and one for the next night before the delivery to help me get the rest I needed. Since I was having so much trouble sleeping, I was going to need all my strength to push her out. I didn't know too much about Ambien, except some friends of mine had to take it every night to sleep. I trusted my doctor and his judgement. He was not only my doctor, he was my friend.

We set the date for delivery, exactly one week later after her passing. He gave me two extra days to give us time to get everything gathered for our hospital stay. I called my best friends and told them I wanted to talk to all of them at my parents' house. They came over immediately and we sat around my parent's pool deck. I shared everything that had happened to me with them at that moment and what the future was going to hold. I had my friend Liz give me a bikini wax which normally is terribly painful but that day I didn't feel any pain. I knew Ellison's coming home outfit from the hospital that I had gotten was not going to fit; she weighed around 3lbs and needed a preemie size. I trusted Liz to get her a new outfit. Liz has good taste in clothes and I trusted her to pick out something special. I am an only child, so my friends are my sisters.

Later in the evening, my mom and I went to Walmart to get a few last things for the hospital stay. As we stood in line, an elderly lady noticed how large my belly was and asked when I was due. I didn't want to tell her that I was carrying a baby that had already passed, so I told her Ellison's real due date which was supposed to be Nov 18th, 2008. I'm actually a weirdo that likes Walmart, because I grew up in California and we didn't have them, but this time I was ready to get out of there as fast as possible.

I went home and started packing for the hospital. I was asked to make a list of everything I wanted done to

Ellison after she came out. I took my Ambien and had my last night of sleep before the worst day of my life. Because Blaire, the ultra sound tech, was my friend, I got to find out the sex of Ellison as soon as possible. We already had our baby showers and had her room decorated—crib, bows, clothes and all. With tears in my eyes, I took one long last look at her beautiful room before turning off the light.

> cabbage?/after care   (Richa)
>
> Please dress her in her PJ's with her hat and swaddle with hospital blanket then the blanket I give you.
>
> I do not want her given to me until she is cleaned up and dressed/swaddled
>
> Please let me feel as least pain as possible physically during process
>
> only my husband/and I present during her delivery/arrival
>
> people can visit while process of dialation is occuring
>
> I have a little animal toy for her too when I give her up for good to go with her that needs to go with her

My private instruction for Ellison after her delivery.

CHAPTER 2 - CODE BLUE

It is now Friday August 29th, 2008, early morning, a day I've been dreading. We dropped Nixon off at our friends, Erin and Jeff's house, and told Nixon he would see us in just a little bit. I trusted that they were the right people that Nixon needed to be with. I slept well. I had been medicated and, as my doctor said a few days ago, I would need that sleep to give me strength for today. We chose the drug that the high-risk doctor recommended to help deliver Ellison. I felt comfortable with this choice as my doctor had told me he would advise his daughter to do the same thing if she was in the same situation. We trusted him one-hundred percent.

When I delivered Nixon, I had a few people in the room with me, my mom, my husband and a few friends. In this situation I just wanted my husband in the room for the delivery. When we got to the hospital it was like de-ja vu of my first pregnancy: I had to be weighed, my blood pressure taken, forms to fill out, permissions to sign, before being taken to my room.

I remember the nurses at my hospital were very kind, supportive and understanding of my situation. My two cousins Traci and Amanda and I were all three pregnant with girls at the same time, and due not that far apart.

My cousins Traci and Amanda, and me

My cousin Amanda had her daughter Amara a week prior to this day, and I had not met her yet. As I lay in my hospital bed, waiting to be induced, I asked my cousin to bring Amara to me because I wanted to hold her during the process. While waiting for Amanda and my other friends to come, the nurses hooked me up to all sorts of machines. They tried to explain the sequence of what was going to happen. I remember sending out a very long text message to all my loved ones and friends, thanking them for their support. I would keep them posted throughout the day. I wish I could retrieve and read that long text message that I sent out.

Amanda arrived from Oklahoma City with her week-old daughter Amara. She handed her to me while I was lying in bed and I started to cry. I did not want to let her go, she comforted my heart in a way that had not happened since we lost Ellison. I could see the nurses peaking in my room with a peculiar look on their faces. One of the nurses asked to speak to Amanda privately. When Amanda came back, she took Amara out of my arms and said she would be back later. I found out that the nurses told my cousin that they did not think I should be holding another baby girl while I was about to deliver my dead daughter.

I believe my other cousin Traci is the one who told me the truth about it and what the nurses concerns were. When another nurse came in, I yelled at her and said it's not up to her whether I hold a baby and I'm not a normal woman in this situation. Most women would not want to be close to another newborn at that time, but I am just different. Amara was brought back to me for a few minutes. The nurses then said they had to leave as the administering of the drug was about to happen.

Ten years later, Amara and me.

The induction drug was described as a faster way for a women's uterus to contract to get a baby out instead of using Pitocin. Now it is just my husband, the nurse and me. It was administered vaginally, I was just supposed to wait for it to do its job. After some time had passed, I asked my husband to lie in the hospital bed with me. I started to feel uncomfortable when the cramping started.

I have no memory of the events that followed that day…this is, my family and my friends' recollection of what happened.

My husband said that within minutes of him getting into bed with me, I was making some sort of a gargling sound. He looked over and my face was blue. He immediately jumped out of bed and called for a nurse, who happened to be on her first day. She pushed the code blue button. All the available doctors and nurses on the labor and delivery floor came into my room and started CPR as I was not breathing. They pushed my husband out of the room and he watched the doctors take turns giving me CPR, pumping on my chest and giving me mouth to mouth.

Usually after about 30 minutes of CPR, if you have not been revived and after the defibrillator has been tried, you are usually pronounced dead. Because my doctor was a friend of mine, he and three other doctors took turns for 90 minutes, with shockers being used in-between. During CPR every rib in my body was broken. When it was not my doctor's turn to do CPR, he called his wife to start praying. He told my husband and my family to start praying. Minutes after that there were emails sent from different countries and across the US, all praying for me. During the 90 minutes of compressions, my IV in my right hand was knocked out and the reaction from that caused my right hand to enlarge to the size of an elephant's foot and turned black and blue.

I would like to share my experience of being dead for 90 minutes. After nine years I am ready to share this part of my story. I remember my spirit lifting out of my body and turning to look at myself in the hospital bed. I thought I was just sleeping, and all the doctors were just working on me.

They say you don't feel any pain while on route to heaven or while there, but I remember feeling sad thinking about Nixon. What I remember next was being held by Jesus like a baby. He held me and he was a giant. I was then at complete peace. It was a feeling of euphoria that you can't experience here on earth. Jesus is just as we have pictured him or seen in books. We looked into each other's eyes. I was told Ellison was safe and he needed her with him, that she was not my child but his. He told me that Nixon needed me. I was completely at peace with that. I had a peak around while still in his arms. It sounds strange but that's how it happened. I saw many children, animals, elders, partnerships of all kinds, people holding hands, lots of smiles. Everybody was just so happy strolling around. Next, I remember my soul returning to my body.

My cardiologist came up with two ideas that might bring me back to life. He administered a few drugs to try and revive me. At exactly 90 minutes all the doctors stopped compressions, stood back, held hands and said one last prayer before pronouncing me dead. Suddenly, I took a breath. I was immediately life-flighted to the hospital in Oklahoma City. Since this was a critical case they did not allow my husband to ride in the helicopter as they needed every seat for machines and doctors. My husband had to drive himself to the hospital. I remember my friends telling me my husband rode with his friend Jay and they got pulled over for speeding. He told the police officer that his wife was in the helicopter flying right above their heads at that moment and he needed to get to the OKC hospital. The officer quickly verified the story and then gave him a police escort all the way to the hospital.

When I arrived at OKC hospital, I had a very faint heartbeat. I was admitted into ICU immediately. At that point the doctors did not know what had happened except that I had suffered a full cardiac arrest and possibly a pulmonary embolism. They knew that they needed to get Ellison out as soon as possible. At this point, she had been inside me for a week after she had passed. My husband said I was awake and the hospital staff told him that I was the first woman to give birth in ICU. As fragile as I was, they had to put a chest strap around my body, breasts, and hand restraints to keep me held down; they also put my feet in stirrups to get into the pushing position. I was conscious enough to respond when they told me that I needed to push to get her out—a life or death moment.

The description I was given of this moment was like that of an exorcism. I pushed with all my might and screamed the whole time. In a short amount of time, our lifeless daughter Ellison was born, and I was put into a medically-induced coma. They noticed hundreds of blood clots in my umbilical cord and placenta. They had figured out Ellison had died from suffocating inside my body and had not been able to receive the nutrients and oxygen that she needed. I then found out that I have an autoimmune disorder called antiphospholipid syndrome, which is why Ellison passed. I now need to get checked every six months for Lupus or MS which is common with my autoimmune disorder. The doctor's told my parents afterwards the chance of survival was 15% after they put me into the medical induced coma and that I had a 5% chance of not having brain damage.

The days before her delivery, we had discussed if my husband was going to hold her. Of course, I was going to, but he wasn't sure. This started an argument, a normal scene in our marriage. After I delivered her I was medically put into a coma and not able to hold her. My husband had to make a quick decision as the nurses were asking him if he was ready to hold her and he said "Yes".
They cleaned her up and put her in his arms and took pictures of the two of them together.

To this day, that is the most loving thing my husband did for me—holding Ellison because I couldn't. My husband was the only one to see or hold her, not even my parents saw her. Unfortunately, we have lost those pictures and I would give anything to have them back.

I was moved to another ICU room and I lay there in a coma for ten days. Within that time, a lot of things happened. At one point my cousin Traci went to my house to pick up a few things for me, and our dog Kaspa, a Rottweiler, ate her new expensive boots and she was furious. My husband handled his anxiety by playing golf with friends, which really upset my friends because they didn't understand how you could do that. I personally do not judge how he handled his feelings as everybody grieves differently. He was not a believer in Christ then so therefore he could not relate to any of the prayers that were being sent our way, and I have never held that against him.

Remember my swollen right elephant arm? The IV had fallen out during the chaos of trying to resuscitate me. At this point it was so swollen that the doctors told my parents it might need to be amputated. My mom begged the doctors to do everything they could to save my arm, "She needs it, she's a hairdresser!" Hundreds of family and friends came from my home town and even out of state to visit me at OKC hospital. The doctors finally concluded that I had had an amniotic fluid embolism, not a pulmonary embolism like they first thought. An amniotic fluid embolism is a very rare condition; it happens during any kind of child birth and has a 10% survival rate. It occurs once in every 40,000 deliveries in North America and is a leading cause of death during labor or shortly after birth.

CHAPTER 3 – TICK TOCK, TICK TOCK

As an only child and being very close to my mom and dad, this situation was killing them. I was told that my dad had made friends with an elderly woman from southwest Oklahoma in the ICU waiting room on the first day. Her son was in the ICU room next to mine. She asked my dad if he had any liquor to share with her, to help with her anxiety as she saw him drinking. My dad went to the liquor store and bought a lot of Crown Royal and shared his Xanax prescription with his new friend. It became their daily routine for the days to follow until he passed.

I had many nurses, but one of my dad's favorites was a dark-skinned nurse. He said she was very beautiful and the way she wore her makeup was so cool. She was also the most lenient with the rules in the ICU unit regarding visitors. My dad somehow stole a key to the locker rooms where he could shower before opening time and pour his drinks in private.

He acquired his own locker, which he used so he could be at the hospital as much as possible. My friend Mandy would leave Hot Rod magazines in this locker to help him pass the time as he had a love for old cars and owned one.

According to my friends my mom was trying to be the strong one and look after Nixon. He was staying with my cousin Amanda, her older son JJ who was Nixon's age and her new baby Amara who was two weeks old. They remember the nights being long as they tried to replicate Nixon's bedtime routine, but he cried all night for his mama. Lots more friends arrived at the hospital and sometimes stayed overnight hoping for some positive news.

One day, my cousin Traci came to visit with her dad. Her dad had recently been diagnosed with cancer so advanced that Traci was now his caretaker on some days. When she came to the hospital to visit me, she would bring her dad too. He was already feeling the effects of his cancer and hallucinating because of the levels of ammonia in his body. As they were walking over to my room, he thought he saw Doogie Howser! Traci had to explain that it was not him, just a guy that looked like him.

Stacy from California was flying into Oklahoma City. She had already booked this flight in advance as she was going to visit me in my home town after I had delivered Ellison. My home town is about an hour's drive from the Oklahoma City airport. Now everything had changed. I was in a hospital in Oklahoma City. Within minutes of Stacy landing she was told what had happened. Now, she had to make a short drive over from the airport to the hospital.

Stacy took pictures of me throughout my coma, while I was hooked up to the machines. I am so thankful she did as I eventually got to see how bad off I really was.

Throughout the days of my coma, many friends brought food to the hospital and wrote kind words in a guest book. During this time my doctors were also doing multiple tests on my brain to see if it was even functioning or if I was a vegetable.

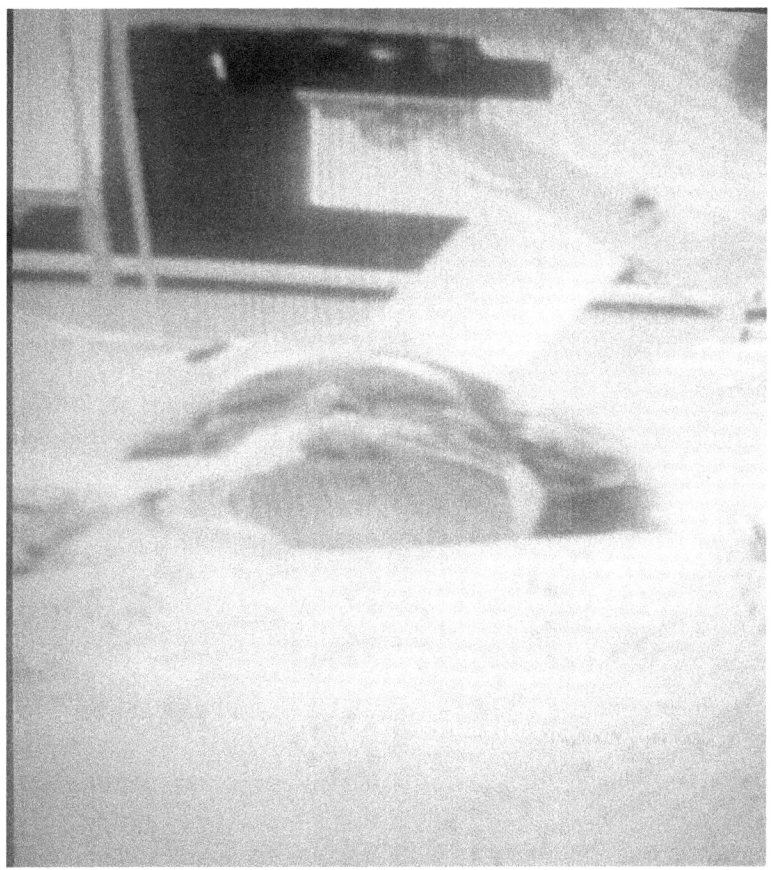

Richa in a comma

> Richie - I love you with all my heart. Everyone in town has been praying for you. ▓▓▓▓ said that God heard my prayer the loudest and worked a miracle on you. Daddy has not left the hospital since you got here. We will soon have you back in Stillwater and at home. Nixon needs his mommy. Be strong.
>
> all my love,
> mom
>
> P.S. You are everyone's sunshine.

One of my mom's hospital journal entry.

The results came back good, but twice when they tried to wake me I did not respond well, so I was put back in a coma. My friends had decorated my room with pictures to try and help my memory when I woke up. Every single inch of all four walls was covered with pictures. As the tenth day of the coma approached, the doctors felt my vital signs were now stable enough for them to wake me again. They warned my parents that if I woke up, I might not know who they were. I might not be able to speak. I might even be in a vegetative state. Compared to the news they had been getting, it was a relief for them that there was a possibility I may wake up this time.

The minister at my home town Life Church had heard about me with the spread of the news locally. He ended up coming to OKC hospital to visit. He instantly put everyone at ease with his aura and calming voice. He brought peace to my visiting family and friends and helped talk with them and support them through this time. My mother later shared with me that he truly helped her come through this horrible experience—of almost losing her daughter and losing her granddaughter. They talked a lot one-on-one and he helped counsel her through the whole ordeal.

It was now time for a third try to bring me out of my coma. My dad had shared his concerns with my friend Mandy. He felt like if I did wake up I wasn't going to be the same Richa. She assured him to trust in God and stay positive.

A medically-induced coma is when a patient receives a controlled dose of an anesthetic to put them in a temporary coma. This type of coma is used to protect the brain from the trauma it has been through. Being in a coma gives the brain time to rest completely and for any swelling around the brain to subside. Doctors wait until the patient has stabilized and there is no swelling on the brain before trying to wake the patient. To wake a patient from an induced coma doctors will gradually reduce the amount of anesthetic until the patient starts to regain consciousness.

The third try to wake me worked. I responded and completely woke up. The kind nurse I mentioned earlier with the cool make-up allowed certain people to be in the room with me and see this special moment. I immediately started rambling off everything I saw in heaven. I started talking about my best friend from college's childhood dog, a dog I had never met or heard about. I knew his name and breed, and it brought tears to her eyes. A friend of ours named Jake died in an accident, I started talking about how great he was doing. Before I knew it, I had everyone in tears around me as I was sharing special memories about the people they had loved and passed away.

My coworker and one of my best friend's Mandy walked into the room. I looked at her and asked, "Is that a Paul Mitchell level 7 OR on your head?" Mandy looked at the doctors and said, "She's going to be just fine!" The doctor asked what that meant, and Mandy said that was a level and tone of hair color that she had changed on her hair since last seeing her. I was fascinated when I realized I had a feeding tube up my right nostril, with my nose ring still there. I reached up to feel my left ear. Many of those piercings had been removed but not the one in my nose. One of my best friends Gretchen told me I kept trying to pull my feeding tube out. To keep me from doing it, she had to lie on me and pin my arms down. I remember one morning laying in my hospital bed and I looked over to my right and there laid an elderly lady next to me, it felt like we had been talking for hours but when my mom came into the room the elderly lady was gone. I decided to share with my mom about my visitor and my mom said there had been no other visitors except her. My mom then believed it was possibly a guardian angel or her mother's spirit that was with me.

    My family and I were given the good news a few days later that I was well enough to leave ICU. I had the choice of moving to the rehab floor there or going back to my hospital's rehab floor. I chose to go back to my home town to continue my recovery and rehabilitation.

    I had a long road ahead. I was not able to walk, tell time, count money, or do the simple things normal people do. There was some memory loss. At this point the doctors weren't sure how much was short term or long term, or if any of my memories would return.

As we were getting ready to leave OKC hospital, I realized I had not showered properly for about twelve days now. Stacy said, "You smell like burnt bacon!" You must love your best friend's honesty! The first thing I wanted to do when I arrived at my hospital was to take a much-needed shower.

As we were waiting around while the nurses were preparing my discharge papers, I started feeling around on my head and discovered a giant dreadlock of matted hair! It was at least the size of a quarter. As most of my friends who were with me were hair stylists, they were able to pull out all kinds of detangling products from their purses to try and get it out. A $32 bottle of this salon quality oil was used on that quarter-sized dreadlock, but nothing seemed to help. I was on so many drugs at the time I didn't care how it came out. I wanted it gone, so I ripped it out. Now I had a bald spot on the back of my head, but to me that was better than the dreadlock, even though I love Bob Marley.

What I remember most from being discharged is my dad wheeling me down the hallway and I kept asking him where my daughter was. He was crying and had to keep telling me that Ellison had passed away and she was with Jesus now. This showed him how bad my memory was—I sounded like a broken record. To this day I believe my dad has not recovered from that exact experience.

I was given the choice to be taken back to my home town in my own car or by ambulance and I chose our car because at that time I was on a mission to get back to normal. I didn't want to continue to feel like a victim.

My husband was going to drive me home but first he had to pick up our dog Kaspa at our friend Lana's house, which was about 10 minutes from the hospital. One of my clients Lauvetz helped wheel me out of the hospital and on the way out she took a detour since we had to wait. She took me to the gift shop to kill some time. As we entered the shop Lauvetz quickly realized the aisle of the gift shop were not accessible for a wheel chair, and now had to carefully back me out so we didn't crash into the shelves. It was taking my husband a lot longer than we thought to pick up Kaspa, and it was getting close to an hour that he had been gone. As we were all waiting, my dad was getting increasingly angry and anxious. He thought I should have taken the ambulance back home.

My husband finally pulled up in our SUV. Lauvetz and her mom Jan helped me get in and made me comfortable before heading back home. I was so hungry I couldn't wait the hour's drive back to my home town to eat, so we called in an order to PF Chang's, picked up the food on the way and ate in the car. As we pulled out of the parking lot of PF Chang's, a car almost hit us; the food went flying. My broken ribs hurt so much as I tried to brace myself and stop the food from spilling all over the car.

When we arrived at my hospital, the deal was I was going to be admitted to the fourth floor which was rehabilitation. On arrival I met Dr. JJ who specializes in internal medicine. I was taken up to my room, I hadn't been given any sort of time frame on how long I could expect to spend in rehab. I would be released for outpatient rehab when they thought I was ready. They said they expected it to be roughly three to six months.

As soon as we were in the room, I was ready for that shower! My best friend Mandy was there with me helping me get settled. I thought I could take a shower by myself, even though I couldn't stand by myself. I tried to hold onto the shower head to rinse myself off but instead I couldn't control it and started spraying the whole room including Mandy. I got everything wet except my body. Mandy tried her best to grab the shower head to help, but I told her I didn't need any help! She said I was such a bitch, which is so unlike me, but she knew my will was to get strong again however, my medicine made me angry.

After my shower I decided I needed to poop. I couldn't remember the last time I pooped but I really didn't want to go by myself. So, I made Mandy stand and watch as I pooped because I was so afraid to go by myself.

Looking around at the other patients, I was sharing the floor with 80-year-old patients and I was the only 30-year-old around. It was an eventful stay, but not pleasant, to say the least. The first night there we all got food poisoning, my mom included. As my ribs were broken, puking was very painful.

On the second day I was working with therapists. My first tasks to master were clapping my hands, watering plants and throwing a ball back and forth with a 100-year-old lady. I thought I was going to go crazy, but I wanted to do whatever it took to get out of there as soon as possible.

Later that afternoon my friend Yong, a nail technician from My home town, came to visit me. I have worked with and been friends with her for 15 years. She came because she wanted to pamper me and give me a manicure. While Yong was there I had another visitor, my friend Carol who was also a client/friend of mine. As Carol walked in I got so overwhelmed I started to cry tears of happiness that I had so many caring friends. Yong gently wiped my tears away and continued with my manicure but was scared of my elephant hand and didn't want to touch it.

That night my mom came again to stay with me. Again, it was so cold in the hospital it felt like 40 degrees! We froze all night and did not sleep, which now came to forty-eight hours of no sleep. I had not tried to walk on my own yet, the nurses would tie ropes around my waist to help guide me and pull me forward with a lasso type of rope.

The next morning I found the rope, gave it to my mom and told her to drag me to the doctor's office as I needed to talk to him. His office was about thirty feet around the corner from my room. I was determined to make it and found a way to put one foot in front of the other while my mom pulled me along with the rope. I made it into the doorway, knocked on it and he looked up at me and was shocked as I was standing before him.

I told him I want out of this hospital as soon as possible. "If you don't discharge me by tomorrow I am walking out of here!" I felt like this was not the place I needed to be. I believed I was stronger than my doctor thought. I just desperately wanted to get back to a normal life. I also wanted to get back to work as soon as possible. I missed my daily routine and my clients. I did not feel like I was getting stronger with this kind of rehab.

My doctor told me the only option for me, if he was to discharge me, would be to do outpatient therapy at a local rehab facility. This facility is an all-in-one rehabilitation center. It was the best fit for me as I needed both physical and mental treatment. I needed to do physical therapy to learn how to walk again. I needed to learn even the most basic tasks like counting and I wanted to work on regaining my memory. The doctor said I would need to be there five days a week. I happily agreed to everything the doctor said. I was now content that I would be discharged, and my recovery journey would begin.

Coming home from the hospital with no memories of anything before I coded, I had no memories at all of Ellison's room. We had completely decorated and finished her room, but when we arrived home it looked just like the office it always was. While I was in my coma Gretchen and my friends completely took her room down and took all her clothes to my parents' house, then turned her room back into the office room it had always been.

I am so thankful that they thought about doing that as I know arriving home and seeing her room could have been overwhelming and a flashback I was not ready for. I'm sure I would have had a hard time seeing her room and all the gifts people had given.

After leaving hospital Number Two, I was about to continue my rehabilitation at the rehab facility. In the early days after being released I had to be babysat. I was also not allowed to be alone or with Nixon without supervision. I was taking pain medication and my memory loss was still a concern and seemed to be a big issue.

One of many medications that I was prescribed.

My therapy at the rehab facility was due to start on Monday. It was Sunday afternoon and my dad was on call to watch me and Nixon for a few hours at the house. I somehow managed to slip away when my dad was on the toilet. I took Nixon for a walk around the neighborhood. I ended up at one of my client/friend Nicole's house. I stood at the front door and rang the doorbell with Nixon standing at my side. Nicole was shocked to see me standing at her front door. She invited me in to relax for a while. We talked for a little bit and it became obvious to her that I was not the normal Richa she knew. She called my dad to let him know where I was, so he wouldn't worry. She recalls me sitting on her couch and I started caressing the couch and saying, "Oh wow, this couch is nice, I think I've been on it before." She reassured me that I had never been on her couch before. She said, "Richa the reason this couch is so familiar to you, is that this couch is the same as the one at the salon you work at!" I got excited and thought this was a sign that maybe my memories were coming back.

Nixon played with her son the whole time we talked. After an hour or so she could tell I was getting tired. It was probably best to get me back home, so she thought the safest way would be to walk me back home, where my dad was waiting for me. He is very lucky I didn't get onto Jardot Street and walk alongside the busy road with Nixon.

My dad and mom had been under a huge amount of stress the last few months, with me being home and about to start outpatient therapy. I think this was the first time they realized I was going to be just fine. They had started to suffer from a few medical problems themselves that the doctors diagnosed as stress being the causing factor. All of my dad's teeth started to get loose and fall out. He ended up needing to get false teeth due to the deterioration of his gums.

Shortly after arriving home is also when the medical bills starting piling in. Family, friends, businesses and residents of my home town came together to help my husband and I through this financial crisis. We had great health insurance, but being in ICU can be costly, the helicopter ride and not to mention the ten weeks of intensive therapy with multiple therapists. Local businesses organized fundraisers such as Century 21 and the Elks Lodge. I couldn't thank them enough for their support. We also had an account set up at one of the local banks, most of these donations we didn't know who they came from. It meant such a lot to us that so many donated.

CHAPTER 4 – ROAD TO RECOVERY

Every day of the week I was at the rehab facility, I think I spent more time there then I did at my own home. On my first day I was told rehabilitation is unique to someone's condition. I sat down with a therapist and talked about what goals I had and where I wanted to be, and with that they came up with a customized treatment plan. I would start working towards gaining the highest level of function that I could. I had many different therapists as I had so many different areas needing work. I bonded with one of my therapists. I needed a therapist for my elephant hand from where the IV ripped out when I coded. Having a functioning hand was important so I could get back to work.

My hand therapist shared with me that her child died in a home daycare accident a few years ago. The usual Richa would ask many questions so I could understand the story, but I did not feel like it was the right time, so I didn't talk or interrupt. She got a phone call to come to the daycare. As she approached, the ambulance was already there. There was a tragic accident and her child had passed away, that's all she ever shared with me. Having both of us lose a child, I felt like we shared a special connection. During therapy we shared many stories and experiences with each other. Other therapists would see us crying together sharing our painful stories. Some stared but most smiled.

You would think a body massage would be pleasant, but because the proper CPR was used on me when I coded, the massages hurt thanks to my broken ribs. My memory therapy was so stressful for me. My therapist laid four quarters in front of me one time and asked me to add them up. I looked down and stared at them for a few seconds. I realized quickly I did not know what they added up to. I swiped them off the table and flipped off my therapist. I was embarrassed and frustrated at the same time. How could I not be able to add up four quarters? If you know me, that outburst and reaction is not my usual personality. Some days I felt as though I was making great progress, other days like these were tougher and reminded me how far I still had to go.

With a great deal of hard work and perseverance, my five days a week turned into three days a week, and within ten weeks I was able to return to work. One of the things that stands out the most from my time at rehab was another patient I met. He was the father of a client of mine. He had suffered a very bad horse accident so was in therapy every time I was. It was nice to see his progress over the weeks and my client at therapy supporting their dad. We would share our progress stories with each other and encourage each other's recovery.

After ten weeks of extensive physical and mental therapy, I graduated from my rehab and was released, ready to go back to my new normal life.

My hospital had put together a party for me to celebrate the life I was given back. There was my mom, dad, my husband, Nixon, all nurses/hospital staff and every doctor that did compressions to save my life. We talked about that day and what they remembered of it and how lucky I was to be alive. I was grateful this party was put together, so I could personally thank every person who helped to save my life.

A few weeks after the hospital party, and reliving some of the events that had occurred, I felt like I needed to travel to Oklahoma City to the hospital to do the same thing and thank the ICU doctors who saved my life. I made the hour drive down there by myself and went up to the ICU floor. I specifically asked for the dark-skinned nurse who had the amazing sparkly makeup. They knew exactly who I was talking about. I told the receptionist who I was and what the purpose of my visit was. The nurse happened to be on shift and could spare a moment to come out and talk to me, we had a long hug and cry. She said what a difference it was seeing me on my own two feet. She then gathered a few of the other doctors and nurses that were assigned to me. I got to say thank you to them all. All the nurses then decided to share comical stories about how ornery my dad was during my stay in the hospital. While thanking my pulmonologist I told her, her face was very familiar, and she laughingly said, "that's because I was in your face multiple times a day during your coma!"

Looking back over my medical records, I realized I had forgotten one doctor to thank, my cardiologist. The doctor who gave me medicine when I had coded. He is very busy, but I did not make an appointment. I showed up at his office by myself, went to the front desk and I asked to see him if he was available. The nurse asked if I was a patient, I said I was an old patient of his and he would know who I am. They said he was quite busy that day and I needed to make an appointment and I couldn't just show up in his office expecting to see him. I told her to please just let him know I was here. She gave me a look like "Fine I'll let him know but he's not going to come out and want to see you." Within a few moments my cardiologist appeared in the hallway and gave me a big hug. I told him "Thank you for being a part of saving my life." He was so glad to see that I had made a miraculous recovery. On my way out, I yelled to the nurse "I told you!"

Months prior to me dying, in our house almost every time I would look at the clock it would say 9:11. It didn't matter if it was AM or PM, I would always look at the clock at this time. After it seemed to keep happening I shared with my husband what I was noticing and how frequent it started to get. He then started to notice this as well. Most times when he would look at or notice a clock it would be 9:11. For some reason I decided to share this strange clock behavior to one of my nurses at the hospital party. She stared at me with a long glare, I knew something was up. She said, "Richa, do you know what time your heart stopped?" I replied "No, I have no idea." She said, "I believe your heart stopped at 9:11 am!" The number 911 has continued to appear in odd and unexpected places, especially with my memory loss when I look back I have found more instances of its appearances in my life. It is also known as the Angel Number and seeing 911 can be sign that your Angels have opened a new door or chapter for you and are encouraging you to start life anew.

CHAPTER 5 – NOW I LAY YOU DOWN TO SLEEP

I am now well enough to lay my daughter to rest and have a real funeral for her, ten weeks after her passing on August 30th. She had been at a funeral home in my home town. The first thing my husband and I had to do was to pick out her head stone and casket. I was still a little medicated at this point, when we walked into the funeral home and we were in disbelief at how tiny the caskets were. It brought a wave of sadness that Ellison would be lying in one.

The gentlemen who worked at the funeral home put us into a private room to pick out a casket. I asked him, "Can I please see my daughter?" As he seemed to be quite taken back by this, I explained what had happened, that I had been in a coma and I never got to see or hold her. I could tell he had great sympathy for me, but he advised that it probably was not a good idea as it had been a while since her death and she wouldn't look like what I thought she was going to look like. I agreed, reluctantly.

The next day we had to pick out the headstone. At this point I didn't play much part in making decisions. I knew I wanted everything to be beautiful, but I pretty much let my husband pick it all out. You could tell that the headstone company felt our pain. I had to hold in my tears most of the day, which was very hard and exhausting.

I called my Uncle Kent to see if he would be the officiant for the funeral. He is my dad's oldest brother of eight years and an elder of the Church of Christ. Of course, he agreed and said he would be honored to play a part in laying Ellison to rest.

A must-do on my list was after Ellison's funeral to have a party and commemorate her short life. I wanted everyone who attended the funeral to come to my parents' house afterwards and have lunch and cake. I called my friend Lauvetz, who was with me during my last day at the OKC hospital and who wheeled me into the gift shop. She was famous for making cakes and I wanted the best cake made for my sweet Ellison. Lauvetz made a big pink and purple cake with Ellison's initials

on it.

The morning of October 5th my husband and I woke up to the day we would bury our daughter. Still somewhat medicated I was able to pick out my outfit quickly. I usually spend a great deal of time picking out outfits but for this occasion I felt like I wanted to be hidden. I just wanted to find any dress that would fit. I tried to put makeup on, but that wasn't happening. Tears were running down my face, mascara was everywhere. I completed my outfit by putting on big sunglasses to hide my puffy eyes.

The funeral date and time was put in my home town newspaper. Apart from family I had no idea who would be attending. As we pulled up to Fairlawn cemetery I was astounded by the number of people who were there to support us. As we walked up to the front row, where Ellison's casket lay above ground, I was glad I had worn my sunglasses. I felt like they were helping hide the pain. My uncle proceeded with the funeral and we were asked to be seated.

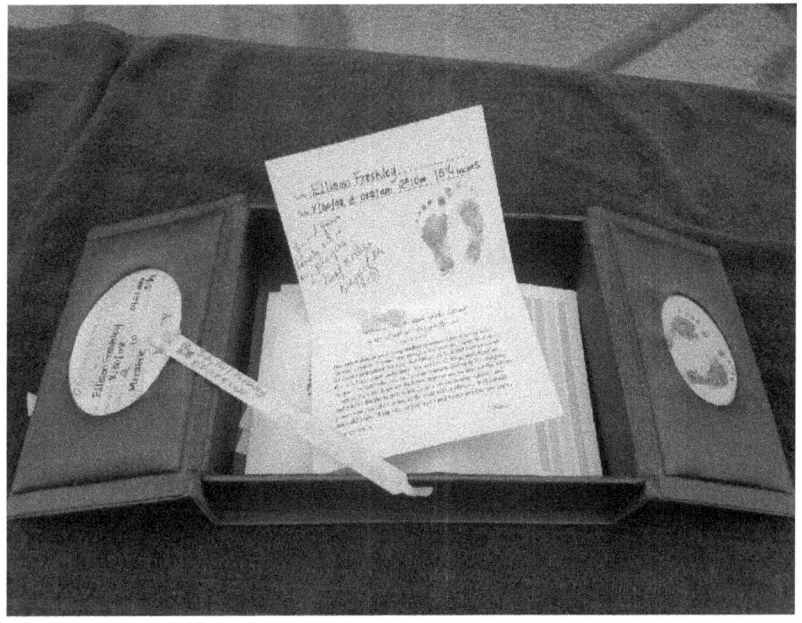

Ellison's Memory Box

In Memory of

Ellison Lazell Freshley

Date of Birth
August 30, 2008
Oklahoma City, Oklahoma

Date of Death
August 30, 2008
Oklahoma City, Oklahoma

Graveside Service at
Fairlawn Cemetery
Stillwater, Oklahoma

Officiating
Mr. Kent Houck

Those wishing to make memorial contributions may do so in her name to:

BancFirst
808 S. Main
Stillwater, OK 74074

Houck Agency
801 S. Main St.
Stillwater, OK 74074

American Heart Association
Heartland Affiliate
P.O. Box 1653
Topeka, KS 66601

Ellison's Funeral Program

Dearest Risha and Thomas:

I woke up this morning with you on my heart. While I know this will not be an easy day for you, I feel led of the Lord to share some things with you. I hope you know my heart is with you today and that you are dear to my heart.

I think the reason it was so hard for you to return to us, Risha, was that you had to be sure your little one was going to be well taken care of before you left. You are a precious, dedicated mother, and the Lord knows your heart.

The Bible says that one day to the Lord is as a thousand years to us. Therefore, when, one day you return to your little one, you will have only been gone from her for less than a day. You will still have time with her, love her, raise her—just in different form. The Lord has important work for you to do here on earth, which you know, and He sent you back to do His will.

Know that in the Lord, NOTHING is lost, Risha. He returns it all to us so greatly that it is hard to understand what His kingdom is like. But He is so faithful to His loved ones. Remember, how special you are to Him, as well as ALL your family and friends.

I pray this word gives you hope, and does not make you sad, sweet friend. Nothing is lost or stolen from us when we walk with Him. I pray He fills you both with His love, peace, and joy. I know the wisdom you have learned through this experience He will use for you to help others one day, Risha. Take heart, dear one. You are greatly valued by Him and me. Feel free to call me anytime.

Much, much love, & In Him,

Judy

Thank you, Judy, for these kind words and asking me every six weeks for nine years when I was going to start my book. I hope you love it and I hope you know how dear you are to me!

Through my uncle's speech and prayers, I suddenly had the desire to open up Ellison's casket and take her out and hold her. I was denied that opportunity at the funeral home and this would be my last chance. I whispered what I was about to do to my husband. He whispered back "Please do not do that!" We whispered back and forth in a whispered fight. I kept telling him that I needed to do it and that everyone behind us would understand. He begged me not to do it here, in front of everybody. I gave in. To this day I have many regrets about not being able to see or hold my daughter. I know that if I would have opened her casket to see her, that all those who attended would witness this, would have been briefly shocked but knowing me and what I went through, I feel they would have understood.

Following the funeral, I had a lot of anger toward the funeral home. I felt like they should have let me hold her. I think the gentlemen I asked should have physically described what she looked like at that time after being kept in the funeral home for ten weeks, then given me the choice if I wanted to see her or not, rather than just saying it's not a good idea. After losing a child it's important to be able to say your goodbyes how you want to, to help with the grieving process. Due to circumstances over which I had no control, I never held Ellison in my arms. I never said goodbye the way I wanted to.

Ellison's Gravesite

After the funeral, a couple days later, we received a phone call that my husband's sister, after flying back home from attending Ellison's funeral, who had visited her gynecologist for being five months pregnant, found out she had lost her baby too. I cannot imagine what my husband's parents were going through after losing two grandkids in two months. Unfortunately, per my Doctor's advice, I was unable to attend the funeral and be there for my sister-in-law which broke my heart.

CHAPTER 6 – BACK TO REALITY

It was my first week back at the hair salon. It was scary starting back with all the issues I had with my elephant hand. Would I remember how to cut hair? I didn't even do a practice run. I went straight to my first client. I am so grateful to my clients for trusting me in those early days back behind the chair. I even had a few clients go on strike, refusing to get their hair colored or cut by anyone else. They just knew that I would make a recovery and come back. Of course, my clients that hadn't been able to make it to the city to see me had a lot of questions, I tried to answer them all to the best of my knowledge from what I could remember. One of my client's conversations led me to figure out who the elderly lady was that had laid in my hospital bed with me. My client was suffering from severe anxiety about my well-being while I was in the hospital. She shared with me that an elderly woman had come to her in her dream, she had reassured her that I was going to be fine and make a complete recovery. My client said this elderly lady's name was Betty. I truly feel like the lady that had laid in bed and reassured me was the same Betty that had reassured my client too.

I was working six days a week ten-hours a day before all of this happened. After losing Ellison and being dead myself for ninety minutes, I realized how precious life is and I didn't want to waste it working such long hours. I decided to shorten my work week permanently to four days a week. I wanted to spend every minute I possibly could with Nixon but without suffering financially.

I knew the next Mother's Day was going to be a rough one so my friend Mandy, my mom and I decided to go on a cruise to celebrate Mother's Day. To turn a day that would be painful into something fun. The night before the cruise, we had to stay the night in Florida in a hotel room, which was so much fun. We stayed up late watching this random celebrity ghost encounters show. One of the golden girls was talking about her personal ghost experience she encountered at her house. One of her deceased family members was leaving her things that she would find. As we're all lying in bed watching this show my mom chimes in and says, "My mom leaves me pennies." So, whenever my mom finds pennies on the ground she thinks of her mom. I shouted, "Screw pennies, I would want quarters left for me, since you don't ever see those lying on the ground!"

Mandy and my mom laughed, and we went to bed as we had to wake up early to board our cruise. That morning we arrived on the cruise ship and all of us had never been on a cruise before, so we didn't know what to expect. Everything was very exciting. They announced our rooms were not ready yet, so we should get a drink, relax and wait until they were.

Finally, we got the call over the intercom that our rooms were ready, and we can go to our room where our luggage should be waiting on us and unpack. I was given the key. I put the key in the door. I had Mandy over my right shoulder and my mom over my left shoulder. I opened the door. About to step in, I saw a shiny quarter lying on the floor in the room. We all three looked at each other and couldn't believe it. I said, "I guess we're not on this cruise ship alone, Ellison is with us." It was the most amazing experience receiving a sign from Ellison that she was still with me. I took that quarter and put it in a slot machine in the casino that night, thinking it would bring me good luck but it didn't. I didn't win anything. I promised myself for every other quarter I found on the ground I would keep on my bedside in a special case that my client Judy got me as a gift. I do still find quarters that appear seconds after they weren't there, it just makes me smile each time and I add them to my collection.

Quite a while had passed and something I realized was that I hadn't even really sat down with my parents and gone over everything that had happened. I had started to regain some of my memories, but it would usually be someone else telling me a story that I would start to remember.

I was finally able to sit down with my parents and talk about things. They needed to share something with me. My dad said during my coma every lawyer in our county and surrounding counties that knew of my situation had contacted my parents telling them we had a medical malpractice lawsuit on our hands. My parents would just hang up the phone on them, as they wanted to focus on my recovery. When I went back to work I had multiple clients confused about what had happened to me. Some thought my doctor did something wrong because what happened to me wasn't normal. You should not go into full cardiac arrest/amniotic fluid embolism after being given medication to deliver a baby.

When clients would bring up rumors or things they had heard, I would always stand up for my doctor. After all, he had been a friend too. All I did during that time was stand up for him. I didn't think he had done anything wrong, the man saved my life for heaven's sake! It was exhausting hearing what people thought around town and that they just didn't think things were adding up. At this point I was still trying to raise my son, work on my marriage and get to back to a normal life. Laying the blame on someone else was the furthest from my thoughts.

Exactly a year after Ellison's passing, the month of August came around again. My husband decided to go to the doctor for a spot on his forehead that he thought was a pimple but now was not going away. The dermatologist biopsied it and said it didn't look like anything to be concerned about. He would let us know the results in a few days. We were on vacation in California. We thought going away during the time of Ellison's anniversary of her passing would help us through it.

My husband received a phone call while on vacation, I could tell by the look on his face it was not news he wanted to receive. That day he found out he had cancer—melanoma and it wasn't looking good. I had a friend pass away from melanoma a few years prior to this, many people do not realize how dangerous melanoma is. We immediately flew back from California to see a specialist cancer doctor and learn what steps were needed to treat this kind of cancer. My husband underwent a blue dye test, which showed that the melanoma had spread to the lymph nodes in his neck. He was immediately scheduled for surgery. The surgery was a success and he was cleared of cancer. He was left with a circular scar about the size of a quarter on his forehead, but the plastic surgeon did a great job covering up the scars from his surgery. I then decided that we would skip the month of August for the rest of our lives.

After overcoming my husband's cancer, we were able to get back to some normalcy. To help ease the pain of Ellison's passing I found throwing baby showers for my friends helped. I helped throw ten baby showers that year and after to celebrate the lives of other babies that were being born. Instead of having any kind of jealously or heartache it brought me joy and still does to this day.

My husband and I had been discussing having another baby. But with what doctors had told us after Ellison died, that me being B negative blood type and suffering from an amniotic embolism, it would not be the safest choice, so either surrogacy or adoption would be the best way to add to our family.

I feel like I am the luckiest person on earth to have as many best friends as I do. After discussing with many of them the heartache I had of wanting another child but being medically advised against it, I had eight friends offer to be a surrogate and carry our child for us. It was amazing knowing so many of our friends would offer to do this for us after everything we had been through.

Before knowing all these amazing friends of mine would be open to be a surrogate, I had seen an episode on TV about the newest thing to do was to have a surrogate from India. I decided to research this area of surrogacy to see if it was something we would be interested in. I was just so ready to have another child, I was willing to look at every opportunity possible. I had a client with different religious beliefs than mine that openly admitted that she did not agree with having a surrogate or any type of fertility advancements as it was against her beliefs. A few months later her daughter ended up getting married and was struggling to get pregnant. Her daughter then told my client she was going to use any fertility drugs or do anything that was needed to have a baby. My client came to me and she apologized for judging me and she realized that, until you are in someone else's shoes, you should not judge. Only forgive. So, I hugged and forgave her.

CHAPTER 7 – THE CARRIER

It's been only a year since the loss of Ellison, but I felt very ready to have another baby. I would do research for hours and hours on the different options that might be available to us. After having so many amazing friends offer to be a surrogate for us this was where we were focusing most of our research.

There are a few types of surrogacy options, and we had decided to have a gestational surrogate, which is using my own eggs and my husband's sperm, but another person carries the child since my body would not be well enough. Due to my autoimmune disorder and no records of my Rhogam shot after Ellison's delivery, we were comfortable that this is what we wanted to do.

We had so many friends offering to be surrogates, how do we narrow it down to just one person? I decided to write down the name of every friend who offered to be a surrogate and add notes about things I thought were important and we wanted in a surrogate. In the end it was quite an easy decision to make. I ruled out people who had health issues or had not finished adding to their own family. The owner of the salon I was working at was one of my friends who offered to carry our child. One the best things if we chose her was that her husband worked with my husband. Every day my surrogate and I would work together behind the chair and my husband and hers would be working together. I thought about if it worked out and she became our surrogate how every day the baby or babies would hear my voice, since my booth was right next to hers. Her and her husband were very dedicated to God, which was also an important reason for why she was the one I chose.

    We chose my salon owner to be our surrogate. The reason I picked my surrogate was primarily that she was done expanding her family. There were no more kids in her future and she also had no health issues during her own pregnancy. The seven others who offered either had rough pregnancies, health problems or were not done having children themselves. I did not want anything to happen to them to disrupt their future for our wants and needs.

I was excited to share the news with my friend that we had picked her. We discussed about how a normal surrogate is reimbursed financially and all my surrogate wanted was all doctor's expenses paid and time off work paid. She didn't want any extra payments for the blessing she was giving us.

In my head there was just no other perfect scenario for why we chose them. Now the hard part, what doctor and lawyer do we use and how does the process work? I love my job for many reasons, because I'm able to see about ten people a day in my chair and I share my life with all of my clients, so I started to ask friends, clients and family who in their opinion was the best fertility doctor in Oklahoma.

I started a chart and wrote down all the suggestions given to me and kept a tally. It seemed like Dr. C was the man we needed to see. I made an appointment to see him and my long painful journey to surrogacy had begun.

CHAPTER 8 – INVISIBLE WINGS

I called Dr. C's office and made an appointment initially for just my husband and I to learn about the process of surrogacy. We drove to Oklahoma City to the fertility building to meet with Dr. C. In the waiting room there were several couples who were struggling with something I never struggled with before, infertility. I am very fertile, I had also suffered a miscarriage at eight weeks when Nixon was only one year old. We never found out why that happened since it was so soon into the pregnancy. The women in this waiting room were on the same journey, just different paths. With clients that have shared their infertility struggles with me, my heart went out to all of them. We knew we were probably the only ones in there having a surrogate. In Oklahoma, I had never heard of anyone doing that, except one lady who did it for her best friend who lived out of state.

There were a few same sex couples to our left and other couples to the right and I smiled at them all. I could tell my husband was quite nervous, but for me it's where I thought we needed to be. We had to fill out tons of paperwork before we met with the doctor. As our names were called, it was standard procedure to meet with the nurse first and then the doctor. I felt like we were at the right place because as I told the nurse why we were there, she smiled and told us a secret. She was a surrogate for her best friend and told us that it is very rare in Oklahoma and that the doctor would be here in a few minutes to discuss the details of that when we saw him.

The doctor came in and took a quick look at my charts. We told them both the story of Ellison and he was quite astounded. He agreed that surrogacy was the best route to take to further our family. We told him we already had a surrogate and he was shocked. I told him the situation and how many people offered and he was quite delighted for my husband and I. We learned a lot that day. We learned that surrogacy is a grey area in Oklahoma, a lot of his couples ended up going to Kansas to make the process simpler. We did not want to do that, so he agreed he would take our case on since we already had a surrogate.

The process was going to be long. The list included all types of blood work from the three of us, including myself, my husband and my surrogate, and a full health checkup for all of us. We were going to have to go together to a psychologist as group, couples and as individuals. The most important part was that a good lawyer was needed. He told us if we ended up pregnant and the embryo transfer succeeded, what we would have to do if we wanted to deliver in my home town. We were told that my husband and I would have to adopt our child as soon as she or he was born and not let anyone know about the surrogacy situation.

As we felt confident that this is what we wanted to do, we shared our news with our surrogate and her husband.

Our journey now had begun. I remember my surrogate having to have a pap smear, a lot of blood taken and having an ultra sound. The doctor seemed to think everything looked great inside her body; she was a great candidate to carry another child. We were then given the name of a psychologist that we were to meet with about ten times. To make sure that we all understood what was about to happen.

I would accompany my surrogate to all her doctor's appointments and a lot of times after the appointments we would go to lunch and go shopping. She even asked me if I would like to attend her church. I of course said yes as I knew how much it would mean to her. I had heard things about her church that made me a little bit nervous, being that I do not speak in tongues. Anything that my surrogate wanted I wanted to do for her. We attended a service and were the center of attention that Sunday. It was quite a small church compared to Life Church in my home town that I attended occasionally. At one point they all had their hands on our bodies praying for a safe pregnancy for my surrogate. Some people started to speak in tongues and I just stood there and let them continue what they were doing. I began my own prayer.

The next step was to the lawyer's office. Dr. C only knew one lawyer that would be willing to take this case on since it was such a grey area in Oklahoma. It is a very small town in Oklahoma where this lawyer was based. Just my husband and I needed to talk with him and learn the legal process of the situation we were entering. When we arrived, we felt like the town was quite small compared to My home town and his office was quite unique. As we walked in, there was one receptionist and we told her we were there to see JP. We sat patiently in the quietest office you could imagine, you could hear a pin drop.

At this appointment I could tell we were both nervous about what information we were about to receive. As we were called into JP's office and shook hands with him, he looked like Billy Bob Thornton. As we sat down in some old leather chairs and looked around the office, there were hundreds of dead animals hung on the wall and it was very dark and musky.

We explained to JP why we were there to see him. He shared his knowledge on what would have to happen if a baby was born via surrogacy in Oklahoma. What we were told was exactly what the doctor told us, that we would have to adopt our own child at the birth. He did recommend going to Kansas to avoid all of these bumps. I told him we had already overcome huge obstacles and we can handle anything at this point.

We left the lawyer's office with a stack full of legal papers. We paid him $1000 on the spot to retain him. One of the papers he wanted me to focus on was a paper that had legal questions which pertained to if I had to choose between my surrogate living or our child living in an emergency situation, which one would we save? Because we know that having a child is not always a walk in the park, things go wrong all the time.

We had our surrogate and her husband over for dinner and had them read over the paperwork from the lawyer and made sure everything was correctly signed and dated. I had to bring all the signed paperwork to our fertility doctor before we began the process of surrogacy. My husband and my surrogate's husband had a co-worker whose wife was a new Channel 9 newscaster and she caught wind of our situation from talk at work.

We got a phone call from her asking if she could follow our story and of course all four of us agreed, because what a beautiful story we were about to share. After talking with our fertility doctor and lawyer about being in the public eye both declined to be a part of the story due to other people's religious beliefs dealing with fertility, he did not want picketers protesting outside of his office. Amy came to the salon I worked at to do our first filming, she interviewed my surrogate and me initially and then she would follow up month by month to see how things were going. It was exciting to watch our first segment which was titled Miraculous Recovery and aired on May 8th, 2009. It was fun watching the segment as they had filmed both at my home and work.

My surrogate and I were the ones that were going to have to go weekly to the fertility doctor for months. My husband would only have to come a few times, the main time for his sperm retrieval. My surrogate and I had to start shots, but my surrogate would be taking different ones. My shots were to create multiple eggs that would be retrieved and then turned into embryos.

With only a year out from my cardiac arrest/amniotic fluid embolism and of Ellison's passing, I was put on the lowest dose of fertility drugs to produce eggs. The average woman produces around fifteen eggs, I was only going to produce around ten eggs due to my fertility doctor being careful about my health.

    I remember the cost of the drugs were astronomical. I had to call them in to a certain drug company and have them shipped to our house. I did not want my husband or Nixon to see me inject myself nightly. I would go into the bathroom, take the needle, and hold it inches away from my stomach. I would have to count one, two, three… I could not do it until I repeated this about ten times over. I knew having another child was going to worth all of this pain, physical and mental. I felt bad for my surrogate for the shots she had to take as she did not like shots. I on the other hand don't mind shots but having to give them to yourself is a different story. The only bad part of giving myself shots was that my belly was swollen from creating multiple eggs and my stomach was extremely bruised where my injections sites were.

    It was now time for my egg retrieval in Oklahoma City. We had finally set the date for that procedure and that meant it was almost time to impregnate my surrogate. I had to go to the city alone to the doctor one more time before this happened. I had an early appointment and decided to call some of my best friends, Matt and Lana, to meet up for lunch after our appointment since they lived in Oklahoma City. We met at one of Lana's favorite places. It was so good to see them and share my surrogacy endeavors. I could tell that something was wrong with both Matt and Lana, they didn't seem their normal selves. They looked at me with a serious look and Lana pulled something out of her purse and slid it across the table at the restaurant. I realized it was a DVD. Lana looked at me and said, "I think you need to watch this. I think this is what happened to you."

Matt and Lana are a power couple for many reasons. Lana is a cancer survivor. When she was five she had a Wilms tumor in her kidney and had to have that kidney removed. She then went through chemotherapy. Matt had a brain tumor and had to have brain surgery when he was in college.

Together they are some of the most beautiful friends of ours. Matt's dad is a lawyer in Kansas and said after watching the DVD if I had any questions to contact his dad. I didn't know what to feel or think at that moment, because I was on such a high of soon becoming a mom again that I felt like something was up.

I questioned them about what was on the DVD, and Matt and Lana said it was a late-night documentary about home births versus hospitals and when watching one hour and one minute into the documentary it was a part of the story that hit them hard because they felt like they were watching me and my situation when I coded.

If you know me I drive like a grandma and I drive the speed limit only maybe 5 MPH over. But that day I could not wait to get home to watch this DVD. I did not want to watch this DVD with my husband. I wanted to have the chance to watch it by myself. Oklahoma City to my home town is about sixty miles and usually takes an hour to drive. I made it home in about 42 minutes. I rushed into the house, went into the bedroom and sat on the bed Indian style and watched this documentary called Pregnant in America.

One hour and one minute in to it, it told the story about one women and her experience of being induced to start her labor. I realized immediately why Matt and Lana thought of me while watching this DVD. This part in the documentary was focused on one lady's induction drug, Cytotec which was made by the drug company Pfizer/Searle. The documentary explained the difference between Pitocin, a common drug used throughout the United States for inducing labor, and the drug Cytotec and their differences.

Pitocin when administered can be controlled if something started to go wrong, like if a patient started having an adverse reaction to the medicine. Cytotec on the other hand when given for the induction of labor cannot be controlled once given. Once it is in your body it vigorously contracts your uterus, there is no stopping it. The documentary went on to share the history of the drug Cytotec. It was originally designed for use with someone with gastric ulcers. Doctors then discovered that when used on a pregnant woman it could speed up delivery time and it was very cheap.

The experts in the documentary thought that doctors who used Cytotec regularly were lazy and wanted a quick delivery by using Cytotec instead of Pitocin. There are SEVERE side effects to this drug, one of which is uterine rupture, heart attack and other ones. The most serious side effect, of which there is only a small chance of it occurring, is an amniotic fluid embolism, which has an 80% mortality rate: 8 out of 10. Two survive. I did both.

CHAPTER 9 – THE TRUTH

After seeing this documentary, I knew immediately I needed to go and get my medical records to see if this was the drug that was used on me. After struggling to regain a lot of my memories from before I coded, I could not remember what drugs I was given to induce my labor. Was Cytotec used to induce my labor? My mind was racing. I thought there was no conceivable way my doctor would use such a dangerous off label drug without telling me all the possible side effects. The other side of my brain was telling me I needed to find out exactly what I was given during labor prior to coding.

I immediately jumped in my car and drove to my hospital, racing through my home town like Danica Patrick. Once I arrived at the hospital I went straight up to the medical records office. I told the receptionist my name and that I wanted to get copies of my medical records. She asked me "Why do you need them?" I responded, "I just need to see them. I don't even need all of them, just the page that shows what medication I was given to induce labor."

She continued to ask questions about why I was requesting my records which I found odd. It was as if she already knew why. I knew I probably had a substantial number of medical records, so I again asked for just the records of what medicine I was given on August 28th, 2008. The receptionist finally seemed to relent and disappeared into the back to hopefully print out the page I needed. She returned with a huge stack of papers. I handed over the fee and she gave me the records. I did not look at a single page on my way back to the car. I sat in my car in the hospital parking lot, skimming through pages trying to find what I was looking for. Then I found it, under induction of labor the word in capitals was CYTOTEC.

My heart started to race. I re-read the page again to make sure, but it read just the same. I started to feel like I couldn't breathe, I immediately felt very hot and my heart was beating so hard I thought it was going to come out of my chest. I burst into tears, I felt so anxious and alone. I think I was experiencing a panic attack. I had never felt that way before or had a reaction like that to anything. I had a friend at the salon I worked at and she suffered from them. She would often describe the feelings she had when she felt an attack coming on. My feelings felt very similar. I always had empathy for people that suffered with them, but I didn't realize how helpless and out of control you felt.

I had so much anger and sadness and a flood of questions in my head. I knew I had to tell my husband what had happened today. I'm not sure that he would quite believe it. He was due to be home from work in an hour, so I tried to compose myself and gather my thoughts on the drive home.

I got the documentary ready to play for when my husband got home. I fast forwarded to the exact point I wanted him to watch. When he got home I shared with him my eventful day, that I had my doctor appointment and met up with Lana and Matt for lunch and that they had given me a DVD that they insisted I watch.

As we watched it together it made me even angrier this time. I'm not an angry person. My husband was so irate that he said, "I knew everybody was right about what happened to you, it shouldn't have happened." That night I called my parents and told them I had news for them and something to show them. We took the DVD over to their house for them to see. They sat there in disbelief. My dad said, "So this Cytotec drug was used on you?" I said "Yes, this was the drug our doctor thought would be best for someone in my situation."

My parents had a lot of friends who were lawyers. They had also mentioned to me a while after I coded that their phone rang off the hook with lawyers from all over Oklahoma wanting to take up my case and that I had a potential medical malpractice lawsuit. One of my dad's best friends in my home town was a lawyer and he wanted me to consult with him first before talking to any other lawyers. I hesitantly called him to make an appointment. He said he could see me the very next day. I wanted to go by myself just him and I, so I could have a clear mind, as I was starting to realize that having my husband around gave me even more anxiety.

 I walked up the stairs to his office and the smell of smoke hit me immediately, coming out of the open windows. My parents are smokers and I smoked in college, so I knew it was cigarette smoke. As I entered the lawyer's office it was quite casual for a law firm. He gave me a friendly warm greeting. As he invited me to have a seat on his couch he also offered me a cigarette and I took him up on his offer. I had not smoked in years, but I was so nervous I thought "Why the heck not!" We talked for hours and smoked cigarette after cigarette. He told me I had a lot of things to think about and there were different options open to me to move forward with a case. It was an emotional meeting, hearing someone else tell me that what happened to me was not right and an error was made. After the meeting I felt in my heart I knew what I wanted to do.

I drove home that afternoon with a lot on my mind. What should my next step be? I called the OKC hospital and had them send over my medical records. I wanted to review them and the huge stack I already had from my hospital. Once home, I started to go through every single piece of paper I had. I had them scattered all over the living room floor. I tried to make sense of what happened that day, what medications I was given and who they were ordered by. After reading until my eyes hurt, I started to piece together the events of that day and what happened to me. The more I read, the more my chest started to feel tight, just like I experienced in the parking lot of the hospital. These feelings of anxiety or panic were starting to become more frequent and I had no control of when they would occur.

After discussing things with my husband, we decided to meet with three other lawyers in Oklahoma City to see what they thought. Did we really have a case? If we did, against who? The doctor, hospital or even the drug company were all possibilities. We also had a telephone consultation with a lawyer in Kansas who was our friend's dad. After speaking with so many lawyers and them seeing my medical records, they were all in agreement that I had a very strong case.

A few weeks had passed since our round of lawyer visits, convinced I needed to sue over what happened, I began to prepare a letter to my hospital stating that I would be suing them. The advice from my lawyer was that we could not sue the drug company, we had to sue the doctor or the hospital. The reason being is that once a drug is approved by the FDA, any doctor can use the drug for any use, even if it wasn't its intended use. Pfizer is a responsible drug company and they did their job putting the warning label on the drug, so it is not their fault that doctors use it for off label use. All the lawyers we consulted with said we had a multi-million-dollar lawsuit as they found in 2007, the highest settlement involving Cytotec was for $26,950,000.

    I tried multiple times to draft the letter, I couldn't seem to find the right words. I began having second doubts about what I was doing. Was this what I really wanted, or had I been persuaded by lawyers? After much soul searching, panic attacks and prayers I decided I could not go through with it. I knew millions of dollars was not going to solve my problems, mental or physical.

CHAPTER 10 – CHAOS

Life was increasingly chaotic. With the recent distractions of medical records, lawyers and lawsuits it was almost easy to forget that our plans for surrogacy were still moving ahead. Working as a hair stylist I not only styled people's hair but at times acted as a therapist for my clients and vice versa. Clients often feel comfortable opening up to me and telling me their problems.

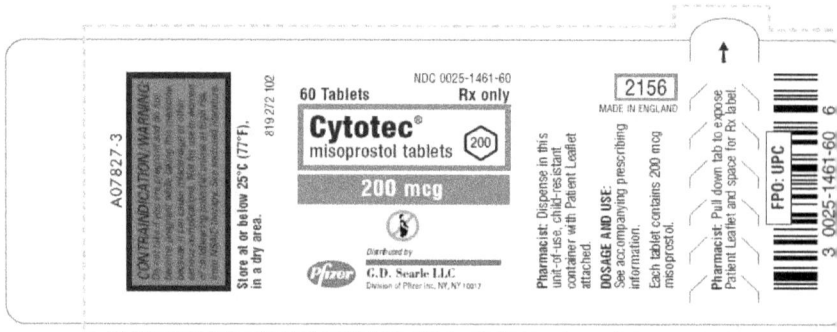

Picture available through US National Library of Health and US National Library of Medicine.
https://dailymed.nlm.nih.gov/dailymed/archives/image.cfm?archiveid=116455&type=img&name=cytotec-04.jpg

During this time, it was hard for me to share my problems with my friends and clients, because I wanted still to save my doctor's reputation as he was a friend of mine and I know he did not mean to cause any of this. He is a doctor, not God and he truly did the right thing possible, so he thought. He had failed me in two ways: 1. Not being honest about all the side effects and how Cytotec was an off label drug and not intended for labor and delivery and its dangers; 2. After I finally recovered not coming forward to me privately and not sharing his knowledge of Cytotec side effects like an amniotic fluid embolism and heart attack, so a surrogate was not needed and I could carry my own child. I know he knew that was a side effect because every health care provider was sent a letter about its dangers from the drug company and there is a black label warning on its packaging that it is not to be used on pregnant women.

SEARLE

**IMPORTANT DRUG WARNING
CONCERNING UNAPPROVED USE OF INTRAVAGINAL
OR ORAL MISOPROSTOL IN PREGNANT WOMEN
FOR INDUCTION OF LABOR OR ABORTION**

Searle
5200 Old Orchard Road
Skokie, Illinois 60077
Phone (847) 982-7000
Fax (847) 470-1480

August 23, 2000   Re: Cytotec® (misoprostol)

Dear Health Care Practitioner:

The purpose of this letter is to remind you that Cytotec administration by any route is contraindicated in women who are pregnant because it can cause abortion. Cytotec is not approved for the induction of labor or abortion.

Cytotec is indicated for the prevention of NSAID (nonsteroidal anti-inflammatory drugs, including aspirin)-induced gastric ulcers in patients at high risk of complications from gastric ulcer, e.g., the elderly and patients with concomitant debilitating disease, as well as patients at high risk of developing gastric ulceration, such as patients with a history of ulcer.

The uterotonic effect of Cytotec is an inherent property of prostaglandin E_1 (PGE$_1$), of which Cytotec is a stable, orally active, synthetic analog. Searle has become aware of some instances where Cytotec, outside of its approved indication, was used as a cervical ripening agent prior to termination of pregnancy, or for induction of labor, in spite of the specific contraindications to its use during pregnancy.

Serious adverse events reported following off-label use of Cytotec in pregnant women include maternal or fetal death; uterine hyperstimulation, rupture or perforation requiring uterine surgical repair, hysterectomy or salpingo-oophorectomy; amniotic fluid embolism; severe vaginal bleeding, retained placenta, shock, fetal bradycardia and pelvic pain.

Searle has not conducted research concerning the use of Cytotec for cervical ripening prior to termination of pregnancy or for induction of labor, nor does Searle intend to study or support these uses. Therefore, Searle is unable to provide complete risk information for Cytotec when it is used for such purposes. In addition to the known and unknown acute risks to the mother and fetus, the effect of Cytotec on the later growth, development and functional maturation of the child when Cytotec is used for induction of labor or cervical ripening has not been established.

Searle promotes the use of Cytotec only for its approved indication. Please read the enclosed updated complete Prescribing Information for Cytotec.

Further information may be obtained by calling 1-800-323-4204.

Michael Cullen, MD
Medical Director, U.S.
Searle

CY20141A

After deciding not to pursue a lawsuit, the only people I told the truth about what happened to me were family members, a few close friends, my surrogate, my fertility doctor and one particular client. As a hair stylist I book my clients appointments far in advance which makes it difficult to get an appointment with me as I fill up fast. I had a client sit in my chair and knowing her as long as I had, I could tell something wasn't quite right. I asked her if everything was okay, she told me that right at this moment she was suffering from an early miscarriage but did not want to reschedule her hair appointment because I was hard to get into, however, I reassured her that anytime my clients have a sickness and have to cancel I will get them in when they feel better. I began to comfort her as much as possible, we talked for a while. I began asking a lot of questions, since I had learned a lot after what I had been though. She began to tell me her doctor sent her home with some pills that she was supposed to take for a few days. They were supposed to help speed the process up of passing the fetus. After I heard that I immediately had red flags, I asked her if she knew the name of the pills that she was taken. She said she didn't, but she would let me know when she got home what they were. She asked me why I was so concerned about the name of the medication, I told her I would tell her later after she called me. I felt that after she had left the salon, she felt better than when she had come in, which is a reason why I love my job.

    Later that night around supper time, my husband and I were cooking in the kitchen and my phone rang. I answered it quickly as I was hoping it was her calling. She told me the name of the drug and I became extremely upset, because it was Cytotec. She was taking it orally, however, in my case it was given vaginally. I asked my husband what he thought I should do, he said "You know what you need to do, you need to tell her the truth." I hadn't spoken to any clients yet about the off-label drug and it's deadly side effects that I had been given. I told her to stay on the phone with me, but to go and get her laptop or get in front of a computer and search the dangers of Cytotec also known as Misoprostol. There was a sudden pause, suddenly, I heard her gasp, a sense of panic came over her. She became upset and was in disbelief that she had been prescribed Cytotec. After she read through all of the side effects she asked me if that was what happened to me when I was sick. I had to tell her "Yes." I told her to confront her doctor and get the answers that she needed because she was not told about any possible side effects of the drug and that it is being used off label.

She then began to tell me she was going to call and tell her mom what she had just found out, because her mom was a nurse and she wanted her opinion. Her mom agreed with everything that we had found out about the dangers of the drug. We both ended up needing new OBGYNs and her mom found us one that had never used the drug Cytotec. This doctor learnt about its dangers when used on pregnant women when he was in medical school. After this incident I realized I could have saved her life by making her aware of what she was prescribed. I needed a way to continue to make women aware of the dangers of the drug, but I still wanted to protect my doctor's reputation, and what had happened to me. I came up with an idea of carrying a stack of yellow sticky notes in my purse, with the word Cytotec on it. I began handing them out to any pregnant women I saw anywhere I was. I told them to make sure that they were not going to be given this drug to induce labor. When I was asked why I just said, "Please just do your own research." I continued to pass these out for the past nine years until now, when this book is going to be released and can reach more women. I will now be able to sleep better at night knowing I have done all I could to make sure no one goes through what I went through.

Knowing that Cytotec was the cause of the amniotic embolism and heart attack that occurred during my labor, it gave me hope that maybe I could carry my own child again. My fertility doctor erased those thoughts from my mind by reminding me that I suffered a cardiac arrest during delivery only a year ago, and I still have a blood clot disorder. If I were to become pregnant on my own, I would be considered high risk and I would have to take injections of blood thinners.

He also reminded me that I was a B- blood type, Ellison had positive blood which can cause complications during pregnancy, if the mother's blood is Rh negative and their baby's blood is Rh positive. Due to the Rh incompatibility the mother may develop antibodies towards the Rh positive baby. If the baby's blood mixes with the mother's blood the antibodies can attack the baby's blood by crossing through the placenta. This can cause anemia which can lead to birth defects or brain damage. After miscarrying, women are supposed to receive a Rhogam shot, this helps to protect future pregnancies from these antibodies that have formed in the blood. I had no record of getting the Rhogam shot, although I'm sure trying to save my life was more important at the time than the doctors remembering to give me this shot. I'm very thankful for that.

Being so advised, after briefly having hope of carrying my own child again, was crushing. This brought up anger and some of my deepest fears. I felt like throughout the surrogacy process I was living with secrets that I couldn't tell anyone about even though I could have if I chose to.

We continued to move through the surrogacy process, it was coming close to my appointment for my eggs to be retrieved, but before that my husband needed to extract his sperm. The sperm and eggs would be combined to make embryos that would be implanted in my surrogate.

My husband was not looking forward to this day, he was very nervous, and I understood. He was called back into a private room as I sat in the waiting room hoping for the best. As he reappeared I asked him "Well how'd it go?" I believe after that appointment we had lunch and had a few adult beverages.

At the next doctor's appointment, it was my turn, my eggs were extracted, and the embryos were made. There was going to be a few days in between the embryos being made and them being implanted into my surrogate. That evening we received a phone call from our fertility doctor that out of the ten embryos that were made, seven had died so that gave us three left we could use that were considered a high grade. We were told we could end up with no babies, twins or even more if the three embryos split. In the legal paperwork that we all signed including my surrogate we were okay with any of these scenarios.

Our fertility doctor did not have much of a personality. He was very serious, hardly ever smiled, laughed or showed any emotion for these past long months of knowing him, but this day of my surrogate's procedure he was completely different with big smiles and talked a lot before he put the three embryos inside her. Being in the doctor's room with my surrogate, it was like watching a science experiment, it was one of the most fascinating things I had ever seen. As my surrogate lay on the bed, I was on one side of her holding her hand and my husband was holding my other hand. The embryos were inserted into my surrogate. It was a very quick procedure. During the procedure my surrogate and I prayed together, it was a very emotional time for all of us.

We were given some paperwork when we left with aftercare instructions and the time frame on when she could take an at-home pregnancy test. Part of her aftercare instructions was that she had to lay flat for 48 hours. After the 48 hours had passed she was able to return to work, we were counting down the weeks until she was supposed to take a pregnancy test. I was so anxious that we cheated a little and took a test earlier than we were advised to. Of course, it came back NEGATIVE.

We waited another week and then took another test, this time on the correct day that we were supposed to. My surrogate took the test, then we both stared at the stick waiting the long minute to get a result. It, too, was NEGATIVE.

I felt my heart break all over again. I had not mentally prepared myself for this not to work. I always had the belief that things happen for a reason and I never blame God for the things I want in life but don't receive. My surrogate's heart was just as broken as mine because she also felt this was what we were supposed to be doing. Through everything I have gone through I always believed that God had a plan for me and I was just following his path—Jeremiah 29:11.

This procedure had cost my husband and I $30,000 out of pocket. Throughout the surrogacy I had increased my hours again at the salon, working six days a week, twelve-hour days just to help pay for it. As my surrogate did not want any compensation, the $30,000 was mostly the cost of the procedures, doctor's visits and double medication. I did pay for all of my surrogate's and I's time off of work and I would buy her some gifts whenever we shopped together.

We had an appointment with the fertility doctor to confirm the negative result. He asked us if we wanted to try again. I desperately wanted to, but I knew there was no way we could afford it again. I sank into a deep depression almost without anyone noticing. I began to build up anger and resentment towards my OBGYN doctor and my husband.

I had never prayed so hard in my life about what to do next with surrogacy and possibility suing my doctor after knowing the truth about what happened to me. Everyone that knew my situation, all the lawyers and all our friends and family, were pushing us to sue my doctor and the hospital. Since I was not in a good frame of mind, I listened to everyone else and started that process.

We knew what lawyer we were going to use after meeting with three different ones. Our lawyer decided on the amount of the excess being 3 million would be the right and fair amount to sue for.

In the next few days I tried to go through the lawyer's paperwork and certain medical records that were crucial in this case. My anxiety was getting worse, having to face all these issues on a daily basis. I got to the point where I felt I just couldn't go on with the legal process anymore. I got down on my knees one night and prayed to clear my mind and not to listen to other people but to listen to God. God told me the only answer was to get answers and acknowledgement of wrongdoing. This meant I had to confront my doctor and try and receive some explanation of what happened that day—Matthew 18:15-17.

CHAPTER 11 – GOD'S WHISPER

I pulled the plug on the lawsuit. My husband was very angry that we got to this point and now I did not want to pursue it. I knew what I needed to do to be healed mentally. I called my doctor's office and spoke to his receptionist who was also someone I knew. I told her that I didn't need an appointment, but I needed to speak with him alone outside office hours and I needed to be the last patient of the day.

I knew what a great man he was, and I knew after speaking with me he would not be able to continue with his day. My nature is just to protect people even people that do wrong, I always make an excuse and want to understand why. Knowing myself well I knew I would not be able to drive myself that day, so I asked my mother to drive me there. I told her I did not know how long it would be, it could be thirty minutes or three hours. I had gathered my medical records that showed I was given Cytotec. I had found out from my lawyers that Cytotec had been banned by a third of hospitals in the United States on the labor and delivery floor only, and on the packaging, it has a warning label not to administer to anyone who is pregnant because of its dangers.

I had a pile of proof that Cytotec was the cause of my amniotic fluid embolism/heart attack and I was in desperate need of answers. My doctor called me back and let me know what time I could come in and see him. We pulled into the parking lot and my mom wished me good luck and that she was proud of me for listening to God and not everybody else. I had prepared a speech on paper as I did not want to forget parts of what I wanted to say to him. I set the font size at twenty because I knew I would be crying through it all and wanted to still be able to read it. I prepared my speech for weeks, this would be my one chance to get a lot of stuff off my chest and also hear the other side of the story. I knew I was ready to do this.

SEARLE

**IMPORTANT DRUG WARNING
CONCERNING UNAPPROVED USE OF INTRAVAGINAL
OR ORAL MISOPROSTOL IN PREGNANT WOMEN
FOR INDUCTION OF LABOR OR ABORTION**

SEARLE
5200 Old Orchard Road
Skokie, Illinois 60077
PHONE (847) 982-7000
FAX (847) 470-1480

August 23, 2000

Re: Cytotec® (misoprostol)

Dear Health Care Practitioner:

The purpose of this letter is to remind you that Cytotec administration by any route is contraindicated in women who are pregnant because it can cause abortion. Cytotec is not approved for the induction of labor or abortion.

Cytotec is indicated for the prevention of NSAID (nonsteroidal anti-inflammatory drugs, including aspirin)-induced gastric ulcers in patients at high risk of complications from gastric ulcer, e.g., the elderly and patients with concomitant debilitating disease, as well as patients at high risk of developing gastric ulceration, such as patients with a history of ulcer.

The uterotonic effect of Cytotec is an inherent property of prostaglandin E_1 (PGE_1), of which Cytotec is a stable, orally active, synthetic analog. Searle has become aware of some instances where Cytotec, outside of its approved indication, was used as a cervical ripening agent prior to termination of pregnancy, or for induction of labor, in spite of the specific contraindications to its use during pregnancy.

Serious adverse events reported following off-label use of Cytotec in pregnant women include maternal or fetal death; uterine hyperstimulation, rupture or perforation requiring uterine surgical repair, hysterectomy or salpingo-oophorectomy; amniotic fluid embolism; severe vaginal bleeding, retained placenta, shock, fetal bradycardia and pelvic pain.

Searle has not conducted research concerning the use of Cytotec for cervical ripening prior to termination of pregnancy or for induction of labor, nor does Searle intend to study or support these uses. Therefore, Searle is unable to provide complete risk information for Cytotec when it is used for such purposes. In addition to the known and unknown acute risks to the mother and fetus, the effect of Cytotec on the later growth, development and functional maturation of the child when Cytotec is used for induction of labor or cervical ripening has not been established.

Searle promotes the use of Cytotec only for its approved indication. Please read the enclosed updated complete Prescribing Information for Cytotec.

Further information may be obtained by calling 1-800-323-4204.

Michael Cullen, MD
Medical Director, U.S.
Searle

CY20141A

One of my many documents that I brought with me to meet with the doctor.

I told him the reason I was there was that I had found out what really had happened to me. I told him to please do not talk during my speech, so I would not be interrupted and to hear me out because it was the hardest thing I had to do besides fight for my life. I was in his office for hours. I believe God was with us during those hours, we prayed together, and I got the apology I needed to heal my heart and to forgive him. He promised me this drug would not be used again on his patients. I asked him to be honest with his co-workers and the dangers of the drug because I didn't want this to happen to anyone else. I told him I would not be able to use him as a doctor any more for multiple reasons. His office would bring back horrific memories and I had lost my trust in him as a doctor, even though I forgave him.

As we hugged I asked him if he was going to tell his wife about today, because I see her every six weeks at the salon in my chair. She too is someone dear to my heart. He said he would have to tell her. That answer was a relief for me because every six weeks I would throw up in the salon bathroom before her appointment from the nerves I got. Now I feel like that will come to an end because of this closure.

I walked out of his office and walked back to my mom's car. I looked in the ashtray and it is overflowing with what seemed like hundreds of cigarettes. I looked up at her and said, "Holy cow, Mom!" She must have smoked multiple packs of cigarettes.

CHAPTER 12 - THE GIFT

As our life was continuing to be as normal possible, as I've said before I share my life with my clients and vice versa. I had ended up sending multiple clients and friends to my fertility doctor to help with their own issues with expanding their family. I got to listen to the heartbreak of one of my client's closure of her fertility path, because they had run out of funds to pay for any more medications. I then remember I had about $1500 worth of medications in our other fridge in the garage just sitting there and I had just the drug she needed. It would give them one more IVF attempt. My husband and I had to realize that another attempt at surrogacy was not an option for us, due to the stress and financial hardship it took the first time. I called my client/friend back and told her I had a surprise for her, she needed to come to my house and pick it up. I had the drug she could no longer afford sitting in my fridge.

I wanted more than anything to give it to her for a last attempt for a baby. I knew she would be at my house in 15 minutes, so I went to the fridge and grabbed the bottle of medicine. I said a long specific prayer asking God to bless her family with a child. She came over and could not thank me enough and we hugged and cried and off she went. I had the best feeling in my heart. I got a phone call a couple of months later that the IVF worked and she became pregnant, because of the medicine I had given her and God's blessing of course.

After letting go of the medication in the fridge, I believed it was time to look at other options to expand our family—which was adoption. There are two ways that you can adopt, in the country or out of the country, and we researched both scenarios. I did not like any of the out of country adoption choices for multiple reasons except one, the Marshall Islands. I was open to either type of adoption but no matter what I personally wanted, an open adoption, which means the birth mom or dad play a part in the child's life, which I felt was important to an adopted child from my friends that have shared their adoption stories. At that time, in Oklahoma, when adopting a child, the birth mom can change her mind a few months after the baby is born after giving them up for adoption.

With the number of people that we knew, my aunt was a principal in Oklahoma City and always told me about her pregnant students in high school, giving their babies up for adoption. I knew we would not have to take the normal route people take to adopt a baby within the State of Oklahoma. My husband was more scared of the mom changing her mind and going through what we just went through, which is another heartbreak of not bringing a child home as expected.

After all the stress we had been through in the past year, there was no way I could have handled further more unwelcome news. So, we stopped there, that day, any idea of enlarging our family. I realized it was not a good idea to bring another baby into this world for a job, we were wanting that baby to fix my husband and me, but that wouldn't have been fair to that child. I believe the surrogacy didn't work for that reason. We needed to fix our marriage first, so we could bring a child into a healthy family.

CHAPTER 13 - SOUL SEARCHING

As the months went by, my husband and I drifted apart. We spent the past year trying to expand our family, but I believe we lost ourselves. He was honest with me about his unhappiness, and one problem was my weight. I'm a fixer. I wanted to fix our marriage. I do not come from a divorced family, but we were throwing around that word lately. I knew I needed to lose weight, but the weight that I had on me was all from my daughter and I was not ready to lose it yet, because in my mind that's all I had of her memory.

I knew I was not ready to shed these pounds in public as it would be a painful journey. I noticed one of my clients losing weight very fast and I asked her what her secret was. She told me about a trainer and a gym in town and I told her I was going to check into it.

July 23rd, 2010 is a day I will never forget. I walked into this private gym which was a one-on-one type of training and I met one of the trainers, named Lauren. I told her my story. I showed her the news clip of what happened, so she could see for herself the images of what I had been through. She had tears in her eyes and I then shelled out $2000 in cash and hoped that was enough to get me started with training as it was expensive. I was an athlete in high school and I knew I had it in me not to complain during any of the hard workouts I was going to be put through. I don't know if this was the healthiest way to get through the workouts, but I thought my daughter suffocated in my body for who knows how long and how painful that had been for her. I got through the workouts by thinking of Ellison and what she must have gone through.

After meeting Lauren, I felt like she was the most beautiful woman I had ever seen. Months and months went by and I started to lose a tremendous amount of weight, still my husband was distant and never complimented my accomplishments, which at that time I was doing for him.

Then the anger set in and I soon realized I wanted to lose weight for myself and not anyone else.

It is now February 2011 and I had lost 70 pounds. I had a lot of extra skin left over, with a lot of muscle underneath. I knew I would never let myself go back to being heavy because, as I said before, that extra weight was from Ellison and depression following her loss. In the weight loss journey, Lauren and the staff at the gym taught me how to deal with stress eating. Instead of eating when I was sad, I ran. People ask how I lost the weight and I must be honest: four times a week personal training, stress, anger, I started smoking at times and that is what made 70lbs come off in ten months.

I decided I deserved a tummy tuck and breast augmentation after what I had been through. I thought I would need to visit more than one plastic surgeon for multiple reasons. The first plastic surgeon I visited was amazing and put me completely at ease. I knew he was the one to do the procedure. I thought I only needed a mini tummy tuck which would have been the size of a C-section scar. I also thought I only needed implants to lift my breasts up to what they used to be. But the plastic surgeon told me I was a candidate for a lift and implants with the amount of skin that was sagging.

The surgery date was set, and I couldn't have been more excited. The day of surgery, while I was dressed in gown and cap, I had a question for the surgeon. I began doing pushups on the ground and the skin fell in the palm of my hand around my belly area. I asked again if all that skin would be gone with a mini tummy tuck. He said, "No, Richa, you would need a full tummy tuck and that the scar would be hip to hip." I wanted that skin gone since I had worked so hard, so I decided to go with the full tummy tuck. One of the reasons I chose this plastic surgeon was because I knew he would not let me look un-natural—his before and after pictures were all natural with minimal scarring. I knew that the hip to hip scar from the tummy tuck would be a sign of strength rather than sadness that I feared.

I was obviously very nervous about being put under, since the last time I was in the hospital I literally died, but I knew God was with me every step of the way. I was told to take a number of days off work, but of course I'm not a rule follower at times and I went back to work way sooner than I was supposed to. Luckily, I ended up just fine.

During my marriage I tried to make things work but we were both still so lost. We decided to see a marriage counselor in the hope that she could bring us closer together. The therapist I picked, I found out later, was more of an addiction councilor, although she did work with marital issues also. As weight gain was a big problem in our marriage, I shared that with our therapist. She immediately seemed to choose my side as she was a larger woman herself.

We continued to go week after week together as a couple for one-on-ones with her. I didn't feel anything was getting better at home. Luckily, we never fought in front of Nixon. He was never around any yelling or disagreements. We just seemed to coexist and ended up living as roommates. We slept in the same bed, but we would keep to our own sides during those tough times. As I began to grow more confident with myself through my weight loss, a lot of things still troubled me.

My workouts with Lauren became much more than just workouts. They were therapy for me. Lauren brought back the old me, physically and mentally, I didn't think that was going to happen. I knew that the only thing left to do, as hard as it would be, was to dissolve my marriage.

I knew who I wanted to retain as a lawyer since I had so much experience with them from the past, and I knew our divorce would not be ugly. The first time I went to my lawyer's office to meet her, I parked in the parking lot but became so anxious I threw up and left. I had to make another appointment to see her, this gave me more time to think about what I wanted the terms of the divorce to be.

During my meeting with my lawyer she encouraged me to be quite aggressive with my choices after learning some details, but that is not my nature. I told her I wanted to handle the divorce my way. She told me I was too nice. We both wanted to work things out with the least amount of fuss. We went to mediation first to try and work everything out and we did.

I got to keep our house, seeing that I was the breadwinner and I did not want Nixon to have to go to two houses he was not familiar with. I initially let my husband stay in the house, and I went and lived with my parents. We thought this arrangement would be the easiest transition for Nixon. My husband moved out when he found a rental house. Nixon just turned five years old at the time, and we agreed to sharing custody 50-50, with no set schedule just equal flexible time between the two of us.

After the loss of a child, especially a stillborn, it puts a huge strain on a marriage. I felt comforted by the fact that we tried everything to make it work. He may have not been the right husband for me, but he is a great father.

We had to go to court to finalize the divorce. We had already agreed on all the terms at mediation. I hated every minute of being in court. The last thing I would want to be is a lawyer. I felt so uncomfortable in the room. Living in a small town it's inevitable that you will usually see someone that you know. I sat next to someone I was familiar with, we were both in the hair industry. In court we did a private one-on-one with the judge in his office. The judge asked both of us "Are you sure you want to dissolve this marriage?" My husband and I both agreed. I think we had a private hearing was because some of our finances were not public knowledge.

To put it bluntly the divorce needed to happen as my husband and I had both fallen in love with other people. I had fallen for Lauren. Lauren didn't know me at all before all this happened. The town I live in is like any other small town, everyone knows everyone which also means most people know your life story too. Especially after what happened with Ellison, if you mentioned my name to anyone they would have heard about it. I loved that Lauren didn't know anything about me, she saw me at my worst and was able to bring out the best in me.

When I told my friends about falling in love with Lauren, no one was surprised, because I've never looked at people's skin color, religion or any differences we may have. I fall in love with people's hearts. Everyone was so happy for us especially because they could see the huge transformation in me. Without my knowledge my friends warned Lauren about the details of what I had endured in the past few years, which put an important thought into Lauren's head. Lauren told me that she would not continue to date me unless I saw a psychologist to help me deal with everything I had been through. I of course agreed with her but was very stubborn about who I was going to see and if they could really help me. I was raised that psychologists have more problems than their patients so that's why I had never been to see one before. After much thought, they might not be good at solving their own problems, but they must be good at solving others. I researched all of the psychologists around town and I also got my friends and clients opinions on who they have used. I knew I wanted someone that had dealt with grief before. I was led to a person who had lost her husband in a family car accident and he had died in her arms, she had lost one her legs in the accident. I knew that she could best understand the depths of my issues. I made the soonest appointment possible with her and began my journey to heal mentally to go along with the progress I had made physically.

At my first appointment I had to fill out paperwork, one of the questions was "Why was I there?" I answered "Clarity" I then was given a few tests to take to help the psychologist know where I was at mentally. As I entered her room she told me to sit in the recliner in front of her, she sat across from me and was looking over my paperwork. She had a peculiar look on her face, she smiled at me and told me to look behind me at the back of the head rest of the recliner. On the head rest was a homemade crochet doily decorative throw that had the word clarity sewn in it. I then smiled back at her and said, "I know now that I am at the right place"

After meeting one day a week, she began to realize that I was one of her hardest clients due to the trying to help me with my grief, when I don't have much memory of the actual events. The final step of my healing therapy from my physiologist was to go to a NICU and register as a Cuddler to be able to hold a 28-week-old baby girl to reenact what it would have been like to hold Ellison. Fortunately, I had the opportunity through acquaintances to go to a NICU and complete my therapy. However, I had to go twice because the first time I went to the NICU, I had a panic attack and couldn't go through with it. But the second time, months later, I was able to go back to the NICU and hold a 28-week-old boy. I did not shed a tear this time while holding him because it was not the same situation of a 28-week-old girl, however, after leaving the hospital I felt complete. This has allowed me to move pass my grief of losing my Ellison to starting my new beautiful life.

Then I had to tell my parents that I had fallen in love with a woman. Even though I know my parents wouldn't judge, I decided to tell them one-on-one. First, I went to my adopted grandparents' house who are clients of mine that I have known for twenty years, both are in their 80s. I needed a safe place to go and a way to practice what I was going to say before I told my parents. I rang their doorbell, they were shocked to see me as I had never actually been to their house before. I asked if I could talk with them and I spilled my guts. They asked, "Are you happy and healthy and is Nixon being taken care of?" I said, "Yes we are doing better than ever."

They knew my parents well and told me I would be just fine telling them this news.

I went over to my parents' house, as I pulled up I could see my mom was in her chair in the garage smoking a cigarette. I joined her and told her to make two stiff drinks and that we needed to talk. Her choice was a tequila sunrise and I sat down in the smoker's chairs in the garage with her. As we puffed away I slowly talked about how she knew of Lauren my trainer and that we have been spending more time together. She said "Oh, has she become on of your best friends!?" I replied, "She is more than just my best friend. I don't just love her, I'm in love with her"! My mom was completely okay with everything. She said, "Well you better go and tell your dad."

I went back to his man cave, which was in the back of the house. We smoked more cigarettes and he got me another drink, we had a whiskey and coke. I told him I was in love with a woman. The first thing he said was "Does she look like a boy?" I said "No dad! She is beautiful inside and out." Both my parents wanted to meet her, Lauren knew where I was, and I called her and told her to come over.

Lauren came over and my dad took her into his man cave and shut the door. My mom and I went back to the smokers' chairs in the garage and continued drinking. We had no idea what they were talking about. We continued smoking and drinking, I'm not a smoker and I was starting to lose my voice and my throat was sore. After Lauren came out of the man cave, we said our goodbyes and
left.

As soon as we got outside, she told me everything they had talked about. She said my dad poured his heart out to her, tears and all, and I've only seen him cry three times in his life. He knew that Lauren was the reason that he had his daughter back. She said that he could not thank her enough and he was fine with our relationship.

Growing up in California, my dad once pulled over on the side of the road and pointed to a homeless man. He said, "You see that man, don't ever judge him, you don't know what he has been through and he deserves respect." My parents taught me how to treat people they way you want to be treated and other people's lives are not our lives and to live what you love.

Telling Lauren's parents, I could tell might be a little bit more challenging. I once had gone to their house because Lauren, her friend and I were going to a live show in Tulsa and her parents lived only twenty minutes away, so we stopped by to stay hi.

Her parents own a house on the lake and when it became lake season, she called her mom and said she wanted to bring a friend to the lake for the weekend. At the lake house that weekend we did things a different way to how I told my parents. I think we made it quite obvious that I was more than a friend. Then we had a conversation with them and her parents were happy that their daughter was the happiest they had ever seen too.

At the lake house, not only did I have her parents to meet, I also had to meet her brother Shawn. All he knew was I was Lauren's friend. I was hoping he wasn't going to have a crush on me as he was newly single, but I think he got the hint.

After telling both of our parents had gone so well, we decided our parents needed to meet. Since I am an only child and don't have a lot of family, I was eager to get everyone together. It was such a great night, and everyone got along so well.

After some time, Lauren moved in, with Nixon and me, and we continued our life together.

My parents, Lauren's parents, and Nixon

CHAPTER 14 - HAPPILY EVER AFTER

As ten years has passed since I coded, I feel my brain has continued to recover, and new memories are coming back. I started to realize, despite how far I had come, I still had some anger issues. I knew my anger was getting worse, not better. I seemed to be angry at everyone—my friends, family and fertility doctor especially. As I was beginning to think more clearly, I could not believe my fertility doctor let me go through the surrogacy process without asking me if I had seen a psychologist after losing Ellison. The surrogate phycologist was just for that situation not my personal problems. None of my friends pulled me aside to let me know that it was probably not such a promising idea to pursue the surrogacy journey right after losing a child.

I decided to ask my cousin Amanda about why she didn't vocalize her concerns to me. I chose to ask her because she is very outspoken, and I knew she would tell me the truth. Her answer was that everyone knew I would have never listened. I was on a mission to have another baby whatever it took, and she was right. A short time after this talk with my cousin, I had an encounter at Walmart. I ended up running into my client whose dad and I were in rehab together. I had heard through talk in our small town that she had also lost a baby, went through a divorce, got remarried and had another baby. In her cart was that baby, just a few months old. Since it had been years since we had seen each other, we realized parts of our lives were similar. As we began talking we both started crying. I ended up pointing to the baby and asked her "Does that help?" She replied "No." She went on to explain to me something that I already knew, but I needed to hear it from someone who had also lost a child. Having another baby does not take away any pain from the loss of a child, nor could it ever replace them.

I have learned through time that God or our past loved one sends all of us gifts that we either learn to look for and acknowledge or some of us don't know how to look for them, like in my case finding quarters. I believe songs on the radio, dreams, senses, smells, coincidences, and synchronicity—all are signs that our family and friends on the other side like to let us know they are still with us. I have a beautiful story that will help you understand what I am talking about.

One day, Lauren and I took Nixon to the park that was close to our house. While there, I saw a friend of mine who I was just friends with on Facebook. I was friends with Matt's family but had never met him personally. We noticed each other and waved to each other and started chatting. I knew he had two girls and I knew what they looked like because of pictures he would post on Facebook. They were both a little distance away, swinging on the swings. The older of the two immediately got off the swing and came over to us. She held her arms out like she wanted me to pick her up, so I did. She hugged me for a minute and laid her head onto my shoulder and let me hold her. As Lauren and our friend Matt watched they had a confused look on their face, like I had met her before, but I had not.

She pulled away from me looked me in the eyes for a while and smiled. I knew then that I was not holding his child but mine. I started to cry and had that familiar euphoric feeling and Lauren and Matt both agreed and were glad to witness such a beautiful moment.

Life moved on. My ex-husband and I work very well sharing custody with Nixon. My husband ended up marrying again and I have become his wife's hairdresser and she too has trained with Lauren at our gym. Lauren and I decided to put our two businesses together and created, Next Level Gym and Indulge Salon and Spa. I run the salon and she runs the personal training gym and Ninja Course. It's a comforting feeling to know that if my Lupus or MS screenings ever come back positive, I know that Lauren will take care of me.

 Lauren has dealt with a lot of the emotional issues that I have carried for nine years and I thank her for being there for me during my episodes. You never fully heal from the loss of a child, but you find ways to cope. I have never had any reason to be a part of any kind of online groups but thanks to Facebook I was able to connect with other Amniotic Fluid Embolism survivors. It is such a relief to know that when I do struggle with issues I can reach out to people in the group who are able to comfort and help me. The only thing we do joke about is my new nickname "Dori" and my right elephant arm is still larger than my left arm, it never quite went down all the way. I was able to get back Ellison's crib bedding. My client used it for three of her granddaughters and handed it back to me after I decided I wanted to reupholster a bench with it, so it could be a memorial to her in my house. It is stunning. In so many ways, Ellison, who began her short life inside me, never left me. She lives on, wherever I am, whatever I do, whoever I am with, until we are together again in God's good time.

Ellison's crib bedding

Lauren and I were married on August 1st, 2016, in the company of our closest family and friends. With Lauren and Nixon, I now have every reason to celebrate life and love, and let time brighten the memory of those faraway days. I have learned that I do not have to live skipping August anymore. It was, after all, the month I gave birth to a beautiful baby girl, and the month that she changed my life in unimaginable ways.

Our Wedding Day, August 1, 2016

Photo courtesy of Shannon Cook

Our family

Photo courtesy of Shannon Cook

My goal as a recipient of an ammonic fluid embolism after receiving Cytotec is to inform anyone who is given this drug about the serious side effects

This is only the start of my journey. I think what I have learned is even though I lost Ellison she is forever with me and God will use this for his glory. I will continue to be an advocate for those who can't tell their story because they are no longer with us. My goal is to make sure policy is put in place to educate hospitals and doctors on the dangers of using this drug off label. The seriousness of the side effects has affected thousands of women and their families. Losing one life should warrant a removal from this drug as an off-label use in labor and delivery.

REFERENCES

Misoprostol (marketed as Cytotec) Information
https://www.fda.gov/Drugs/DrugSafety/ucm111315.htm

Cytotec FDA warning label
https://www.accessdata.fda.gov/drugsatfda_docs/label/2009/019268s041lbl.pdf

Tatia Oden French
Memorial
Foundation
https://tatia.org/

Tatia Story Documentary
https://www.youtube.com/watch?v=7-wPXJCwU2o
https://www.youtube.com/watch?v=ww9hLz_vchs

Tatia DC Event: Role of the Birthing Community in Improving U.S. Maternity Care
https://www.youtube.com/watch?v=r5aStMnzVFs

The Freedom to Birth—The Use of Cytotec to Induce Labor: A Non-Evidence-Based Intervention
https://www.ncbi.nlm.nih.gov/pmc/articles/PMC2684033/

Next page: some of my personal medical records.

DISCHARGE SUMMARY

FRESHLEY, RICHA RENEE
PATIENT #:

ACCOUNT #:
DATE OF ADMISSION: 08/29/08
DATE OF DISCHARGE: 09/09/08

cc:
Cc:

DISCHARGE FROM OBSTETRICAL CARE: 09/01/08

HISTORY OF PRESENT ILLNESS:
The patient was admitted to the intensive care unit as a transfer from Dr. _____ in Stillwater. The patient was admitted as a 30-year-old white female, gravida 3-1-0-1-1 at approximately 28-29 weeks gestation with an intrauterine fetal demise, complicated by a postadmission cardiorespiratory arrest. The patient has what may have been an amniotic fluid embolus during her induction process with Cytotec. At the time of induction and the event her membranes were intact and her cervix was approximately 3 cm after cervical ripening with Cytotec at varying doses inclusive of 25 mcg every 4 hours and 100 mcg every 6 hours. She had an intrauterine demise with some evaluation already performed at the transferring site inclusive of weekly positive IgM anticardiolipin antibodies. The patient was transferred after a cardiorespiratory arrest for which she went PEA and was subsequently revived. She was transferred as a ventilated patient with coagulopathy. She had an evaluation of her cardiorespiratory system inclusive of spiral CAT scan which did not appear to show evidence of pulmonary embolus, echocardiography which showed essentially normal left ventricular function and an ejection fraction estimated at 50-60% (although the study was somewhat limited) and evidence of pleural and abdominal fluid and possible hilar infiltrates on abdominal and chest studies.

Maternal fetal medicine and pulmonary services were involved in the patient's care inclusive of myself, Dr. _____ and Dr. _____. The patient received blood products for correction of her coagulopathy (she had received a thrombolytic agent prior to transfer), packed red blood cells for anemia and multiple doses of Lasix and Albumin. She also had various electrolytes replaced. Cardiac enzymes were elevated which was felt most likely related to the resuscitative event and it was felt a low likelihood that the patient had a myocardial infarction. Intracranial imaging was essentially unremarkable. Once relatively stable in the intensive care unit the patient was evaluated for an induction process of labor. Membranes were ruptured with bloody fluid noted. The fluid was somewhat foul-smelling. The patient was 3 cm dilated at the time of the induction process. She progressed into active labor fairly quickly and did not require any uterotonic agents. She went on to have a spontaneous vaginal delivery of a demised and somewhat macerated fetus which appeared to be phenotypically female. Apgars were obviously 0, 0 and 0 at 1, 5 and 10 minutes respectively. The birthweight was approximately 2

HISTORY AND PHYSICAL

FRESHLEY, RICHA RENEE
PATIENT #: J0793705

25.8 seconds. Lupus anticoagulant testing was negative. The patient did have positive IgM anticardiolipin antibodies at 14.8 MPL. IgG anticardiolipin antibodies were negative at 5.1 GPL. The patient was reportedly normotensive and afebrile at presentation. Based on review of records available, the patient received Cytotec at 25 mcg per vagina every 4 hours which was subsequently changed to Cytotec at 100 mcg per vagina every 6 hours. Induction alternatives and agents for utilization were reviewed with Dr.   on the date of phone consultation. Based on the records available for review during the induction process there was no obvious hyper- or hypotension. The patient did appear to have received an epidural. As best I can tell from the record her initial vital signs showed a blood pressure of 119/67, a pulse of 94, respiratory rate of 20, and a temperature 98.6 degrees Fahrenheit. The cervix was clinically closed and thick. Later that day by approximately 3:00 p.m. the cervix was fingertip and 50% effaced and at that time Cytotec was increased to 100 mcg. Based on the records the patient on arrival was not reporting any pain. The patient was reportedly doing well up until the morning of the event, which was earlier today. Her partner, the father of the baby, was present with her at the time of the event. Dr.   had just seen the patient at approximately 9:00 a.m. The cervix was reportedly 3 cm dilated and he was considering artificial rupture of membranes but had not as of yet done so as the cervix was somewhat anterior. The father of the baby reports that the patient was somewhat groggy and at approximately 9 to 9:30 a.m. started having difficulty breathing. At some point her color changed from a reddish to blue and her eyes reportedly rolled back into her head and she became unresponsive, collapsing back in bed. At this time nursing staff were called and a CODE BLUE was called. The patient had an extensive code performed and the code history was reviewed. The code was called at approximately 0900 or 0920 with CPR administered. The initial rhythm was reported as PEA and later became a sinus tachycardia after CPR, atropine, Narcan, and bicarbonate. The patient also received epinephrine. She had a fingerstick blood sugar at this time of approximately 121 mg/dL. The patient had several other rounds of epinephrine and bicarbonate and eventually proceeded into V-tach. She was intubated at some point and underwent multiple medical treatments inclusive of several other rounds of bicarbonate, epinephrine and eventually Levophed for maintenance of pressure. Although at some point she was a sinus tachycardia, there were several periods, at least 1 hour into the code, at which she was pulseless. She was treated with an epinephrine drip and dopamine in addition to the aforementioned agents and Levophed. At least throughout some portion of this resuscitation she did demonstrate some marked hypertension with several pressures noted to be as high as 230 systolic and low 100s diastolic. Ativan and Diprivan were additionally given. Her epidural had been discontinued early on in the aforementioned resuscitative effort. Of note during her induction process she was additionally treated with Tylenol, Zofran, Lomotil and Demerol as needed. Her initial blood gas available for review showed a pH of 6.979 with a pCO2 of 56.9 and a pO2 of 97.8. Oxygen saturation was 91.8. That gas was somewhat into the code. Her initial gas performed at approximately 920 which would have been just at the time that the code was called and probably her first arterial blood gas performed showed a pH of 7.28 with a pCO2 of 40.9, a pO2 of 36.5, a bicarbonate of 18.8, a base excess of -7.5 and an oxygen saturation of 56%. This is likely the original blood gas performed demonstrating a marked hypoxia and acidosis. Once stabilized Dr.   called with a request to

ICUC

HISTORY AND PHYSICAL

FRESHLEY, RICHA RENEE
PATIENT #: J0793705

ACCOUNT #:
DATE OF ADMISSION: 08/29/08

MICUC 1
                                    Referring Physician

CHIEF COMPLAINT:
Unresponsive; transferred from Stillwater.

HISTORY OF PRESENT ILLNESS:
Ms. Freshley is a 30-year-old white female who is transferred from Stillwater secondary to a full arrest. She is 28-week gestation with fetal demise that was admitted to Stillwater for delivery of the fetus when she went into full arrest. The code lasted approximately an hour and 10 minutes. The patient was given some Cytotec to induce labor. The code happened approximately an hour or so after the injection. The patient just returned from a trip to California over the weekend and Monday was not feeling well. Tuesday she went to her OB's office to be checked and that is when they found that the fetal demise was present. She was scheduled to come in on Thursday for induction. The patient is currently unresponsive and all the information is obtained from the limited Stillwater chart and the parents who are in the room. The husband is on his way.

PAST MEDICAL HISTORY:
The patient has no past medical history, no surgical history.

SOCIAL HISTORY:
She has got a 2-year-old son. She is Rh negative. She is not a smoker nor does she abuse any alcohol. She is allergic to Erythromycin and hydrocodone.

FAMILY HISTORY:
Noncontributory.

PHYSICAL EXAMINATION:
GENERAL: She is unresponsive on the ventilator and on Levophed. LUNGS: She has bilateral coarse wheezes. HEART: Tachycardic and regular. ABDOMEN: She has got a gravid uterus. She has bowel sounds. She has no edema.

DATA:
Chest x-ray from Stillwater is clear. The chest x-ray here is pending. Labs here are pending. Her ABG here is 7.39, 35, and 367 on assist control of 100%. The only lab she had in Stillwater was a CBC and her white blood cell count there was 44,800. She also had numerous ABGs done during the code.

IMPRESSIONS AND RECOMMENDATIONS:
1. Septic shock status post arrest. Etiology of this is as of yet unclear;

HISTORY AND PHYSICAL

FRESHLEY, RICHA RENEE
PATIENT #: J0793705

however, I have to suspect that it has something to do with the fetal demise and the induction therapy. Did she have amniotic fluid emboli? She was hypoxic at the time. She is no longer hypoxic at this point. The family states that it happened shortly after they broke her water there. The order of events is somewhat unclear. She is currently on pressors. I will pan culture her, start her on imipenem, and check for DIC. For coagulopathy she was given some Retavase there. They were suspecting an embolism. She has recently returned from a trip to California where she was on the plane so a pulmonary embolism is, of course, in the differential. I am getting a spiral CT to rule this out.

2. Retained fetus. _____ knows about this patient and will see her and I believe that this is likely the source of her sepsis. Will defer to him for further treatment of this process.

3. Respiratory failure. She is on _____. The acidosis has resolved. Will continue this for now. Will continue this for now.

4. Hypotension secondary to shock. She is on Levophed and she is responding nicely to it. An echocardiogram is pending. Will check a CT scan of her thorax as well as a spiral CT to make sure that she is intact. Will also get an echocardiogram to check for cardiomyopathy versus pericarditis, et cetera. Continue her workup. Her heart rate is elevated. I suspect that this is all a part of the overall septic shock picture. Will watch this very closely. Will use amiodarone and involve Cardiology if necessary. I have discussed with the family the prognosis is very guarded. Will make further assessments and recommendations as necessary.

#1226779

<<Signature On File>>

0829-0252
MBAUNA   MJM
D: 08/29/08 1512
T: 08/29/08 1711

Thank you to Christy Story and Jody Harris for making my story come to life.

Richa and Christy

Richa and Jody

Book cover photos were taken courtesy of Sarah Little.

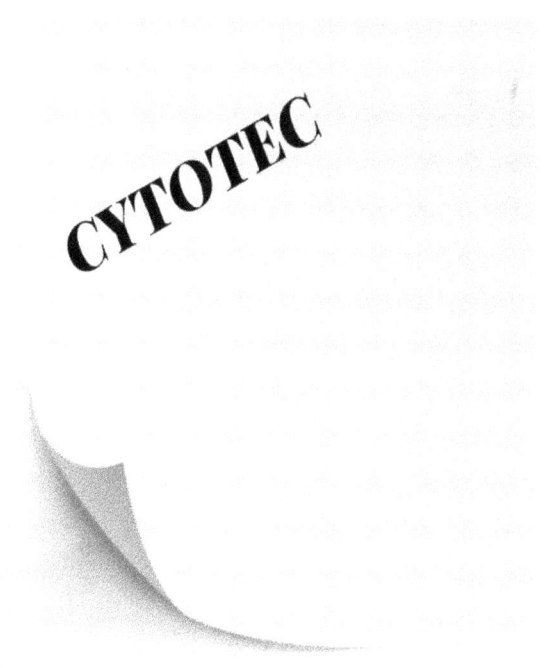

I know from past experience, that anger has to be channeled into productive modes because anger itself is not necessarily productive. Tatia mother, Maddy Oden

I dedicate this book to Ellison and Nixon my beautiful children who give me strength to tell my story. Also, to Tatia, her baby Zora, and many others who were victims of Cytotec's off label use.

www.ingramcontent.com/pod-product-compliance
Lightning Source LLC
Chambersburg PA
CBHW070153100426
42743CB00013B/2893